A Wildflower is Often Overlooked

Intentionally Planted by God

Melanie McKay

Contents

Hello! My name is Melanie, and this is my story.

I consider myself a wildflower, and most of my life I felt overlooked. However, after learning who I was in Him, I understand that I was intentionally planted by God. A glimpse into my life: it's terrifying to think about someone reading this, let alone telling perfect strangers encounters of my life. They are raw, real, and revealing, but this is me. All the good, the bad, and the unreal situations that have taken place over my life. Why would I reveal so much about myself to a world full of strangers? To a world full of judgment and condemnation? That's an excellent question, and I am happy to tell you.

If this book reaches only one person, changes only one person's life, then laying it all out there will be worth it. Everything I have endured, every mortifying mistake I have made, and every good, right choice I picked along the way was for you. I dedicate this book to you, Reader. I hope this helps you along the way to know that you are not the sum of what you have done but that you are loved- yesterday, today, and tomorrow. I don't know you, but I am praying for you through this journey of 52 weeks.

I want to thank my daughters Amber & Kelli who wouldn't let me give up and encouraged me through this process of doubt and insecurities while speaking life into me. To my friends Sara & Renee for pushing me to publish and holding me accountable to the things I want to accomplish. To my husband for always believing in me and reminding me that my testimony will be a light to others so that they don't feel alone in this journey. Lastly, thank you to Ashley & Sara for the artwork and book cover work. You ladies are amazing!!

We are all a little messy; let your mess be His message.

Always, Melanie

Foreword

What do wildflowers have to do with this devotional? Wildflowers are the only flowers that bloom where the seed lands. A wildflower doesn't need to be planted like other flowers by man… it just grows where it sees fit. A wildflower is intentionally planted by God. A wildflower grows, blooms, and is beautiful exactly in the place God put it. Therefore, I proclaim myself as a wildflower. If you are anything like me, you too are a wildflower and are intentionally planted by God. You didn't pick up this book by accident. Something made you pick up this book, and that is going to change your life.

I wrote this devotional and journaling book because God told me to. Plain and simple, that's the answer. How I got to actually writing it is a different story. I was asked by women's ministry leadership in my church to write a devotional for our Mother's Day devotional book. This is how it began. I wrote the devotional (which is in this book, actually,) and after writing it, I realized that I really enjoy writing. At this very time, we were also transitioning from being youth pastors for 18 years into a different ministry discipling young adults. Knowing my role was going to be quite different and being unsure where I would fit into this new season felt daunting. It sounds like it would be similar, but it's a totally different animal. I knew the part I played in youth ministry, but I was unsure of who I was apart from that. There was personal family stuff happening that many were unaware of, and I was being pulled emotionally in several different directions. I was feeling very overwhelmed and started to shut down. I took a week to fast, pray, and lean on God to speak to me, and wouldn't you know… He did. He told me to write a book. I laughed! That doesn't answer my questions! What a joker He is! However, He wasn't kidding. He showed me I needed to write a devotional and all the little details even down to the fact that every devotional is going to be a testimony of my life and where He was in those moments. These are actual stories from my life, how I got through things, and where God was during them. I thought, *That's a great idea! However, who wants to hear stories of my life? I am just me, Lord.* God said to me, "They do.

They need it. It will help save, heal, and set people free. That was enough for me.

So I started this journey from every memory that I can possibly think of. Along this journey, God has also shown me where he was in every single situation, and this has brought healing to me first and foremost. At the end of every week, you will also be writing down seven things you are thankful for. Doing this is going to help fight anxiety and depression because when you are constantly aware of what you are thankful for, you are verbally and physically fighting the enemy's lies. This is good for our mental and physical health. I recently read many articles stating that there is a growing body of research on the benefits of being thankful. These studies have found that giving thanks can help people sleep better, lower stress, and improve relationships. There are also findings that it can lower your risk of heart disease and symptoms of depression and anxiety. I'm glad the world is catching up with what we already knew through Jesus.

Our words and thoughts either build a palace for us to live in or a prison to hold us captive. The choice is yours. If we know who we are, it doesn't matter who we are not.

"But you are a chosen people, a royal priesthood, a holy nation, God's special possession, that you may declare the praises of him who called you out of darkness into his wonderful light." 1 Peter 2:9 NIV

"Now to him who is able to do immeasurably more than all we ask or imagine, according to his power that is at work within us," Ephesians 3:20 NIV

"But God demonstrates his own love for us in this: While we were still sinners, Christ died for us." Romans 5:8 NIV

"…and even if not, He's still good" Daniel 3:18

How to use this book? Read the devotional testimonies, then daily read the scripture and journal what it means to you and how you will apply it to your life. Enjoy the journey.

Week 1: Freedom

"Do not conform to the pattern of this world, but be transformed by the renewing of your mind." - Romans 12:2

"We demolish arguments and every pretension that sets itself up against the knowledge of God, and we take captive every thought to make it obedient to Christ." - 2 Corinthians 10:5

What is freedom? When you hear the word freedom, what does that mean to you? You might think of the Fourth of July, or that we live in a free country where we're free to drink whatever we want or choose the food we want to eat and we're free to get in our vehicles and go anywhere we want to go. That's not the kind of freedom I'm talking about. I'm talking about spiritual freedom. Freedom in our minds to the point of no longer listening to the lies of the enemy. We can find freedom in Christ once we recognize the lies that hold us captive. It's truly eye-opening. That moment when you see something for the very first time even though you've seen it a million times before. I've hidden myself away for so long believing lies. There were so many layers of blinders that it's now a process to remove them. I am removing them one by one. Sometimes it's painful and scary. The enemy works very hard to keep us captive and lost. Many times, you cannot tell what someone may be dealing with by what's going on on the outside. It just may be what's going on on the inside. So many times you try to hide it and cover it up but you can feel it trying to explode. You try to hide those insecurities even more, sometimes to the point of isolation.

I was reading a devotional on my Bible app. This may seem a little like *Inception* but instead of a dream within a dream, it's a devotional within a devotional. Here we go. This devotional was talking about truth and freedom, much like I am today. It talked about how there is a spiritual force trying to lure us into the world of lies, and once we fall for those lies we create an atmosphere around us from which we operate and see our own lives. From that stems how we see things like social media, news, family, and unplanned things that happen daily that push our buttons and may push us to the point of exploding. When we are squeezed, what comes out? Is it peace, love, and joy, or is it anger, fear, or frustration? He goes on to talk about spiritual freedom. I'm going to share with you how I got there, and I'm hoping by sharing this that it doesn't take you as long as it's taken me.

I've walked around for many years believing lies, and I didn't even realize I was believing them. I was completely blinded. I've been in ministry since 2000. I'm writing this in 2019. I have only recently started letting go of these lies that I didn't know I was holding onto. When you are in ministry for so many years, it's very easy to hide there. I appeared confident and put together (mostly). I know what truth to tell people, I know and believe God's word and what it says about our values in our purpose. It was and is easy for me to encourage people in this. What I didn't know was that I was believing a lie that I wasn't good enough to be in a certain circle of people or I wasn't the right kind of cool mom or woman to do certain things within the church. For so long I have felt like I have been in the shadow of my husband, and I was comfortable there. When I would speak up, I always felt shut down or that my idea wasn't valued, so I would just stay silent. Once we transitioned from youth pastors to full-time Associate and Freedom Center Academy pastors, something switched within me. I knew my new assignment. I started letting go of these lies that I didn't know I was holding onto. But where does my freedom come from? Where is my place now? Do I stay in the shadow of my pastor husband or is it time to speak out and do what God is whispering in my ear? I've heard His sweet voice before and I would always explain it away. Now... now is the time!! It's time for me to be free!! God placed it on my heart to write a devotional and journaling book. I've never written a devotional before, let alone a whole book of them. I said yes. And here we are. We can't receive freedom from truth until we are aware of the lies we are believing. What lies are you believing about yourself?? I hope your journey through this devotional book helps you find what God has for you. Freedom!!

"Now the Lord is the spirit, and where the Spirit is, there is freedom." 2 Corinthians 3:17

1. What lies are you believing about yourself?
2. Begin to pray about who you will confide in about the lies you believe about yourself.
3. What truth does God say about you that replaces the lies that you believed?
4. The truths that replaced the lies that you believed will be added to the list of things you will tell the person you're confiding in. What tangible thing can you do daily to remind you of the truth that God says about you?
5. What steps can you take to walk in true spiritual freedom? What is God speaking to you about spiritual freedom?

Read and Journal.
Day 1: John 8:36
Day 2: Galatians 5:13-14
Day 3: Galatians 5:1
Day 4: Psalms 119:45
Day 5: Ephesians 3:12
Day 6: Acts 13:38-39
Day 7: Romans 6:22

Today's the day that you will call your mentor/person you are going to confide in and you are going to tell them the lies that you've been believing about yourself and the truth that you are replacing that lie with. Ask this person to pray with you and encourage you during this journey in finding spiritual freedom.

Write down one thing each day that you are thankful for.

Week 2: Safety

When I was a little girl, my mother and I used to go to a church in the town over from us. I remember we would go every Sunday and I would go into the kids' area and I would play with all the toys and other children. I remember crying and being so sad that I was away from my mother and I also remember that I wanted to ride on the rocking horse because I had one at home and that was the only thing in the room that made me feel safe. Probably because it was familiar. I remember crying to the point that they had to get my mother and I remember going with her into big service (that's what I called it) and sitting with her. I remember sitting on her lap and feeling so safe and away from what was scary in the other room. I know now as an adult that there was literally nothing scary in the other room. I even remember the workers being very nice and trying to calm this crying child. All I remember is that I didn't feel safe away from my mother. Just like this story, which is true, by the way. I feel like this is how we should be with our relationship with God. When we are in relationship with God, we are safe, and we feel safe and we are close to him. When we are not in relationship with God we do not feel safe and we feel afraid, lonely, and disconnected, and just like my story when we cry out for our Father he's there just like my mother was. I'll even go as far as saying our Father is there even when our earthly mother and father are not. There is a protection and safety in relationship with God. He loves us. He loves us more than the birds of the air and he takes care of them and they never lack for anything. When I am scared or I'm crying, I know that I can sit on my heavenly Father's lap and feel safe again. We are created in his image, that's why our parents are created to nurture us just as He does. I apologize if you didn't grow up having a mother or a father that nurtured you but I promise you that your heavenly Father does and will if you let him. It starts at the point of letting Him.

"May the LORD answer you when you are in distress; may the name of the God of Jacob protect you." - Psalms 20:1

Read and Journal.
Day 1: 1 Corinthians 10:13
Day 2: Deuteronomy 31:6
Day 3: Isaiah 41:10
Day 4: Proverbs 2:11
Day 5: Proverbs 4:6
Day 6: Psalms 5:11
Day 7: Psalms 34:19

Write down one thing each day that you are thankful for.

Week 3: Jesus, Please Let My Fish Live

It was March 1976, and I was three years old. I'm so surprised that I can remember this. My mom had to fill me in with the details because my three-year-old brain was only worried about my fish that I had with me. My mom told me that we had a bad ice storm that year. After 5 days of being at home without power we packed up to go to my grandma's where they had power. I was sitting in the front passenger seat with a fishbowl on the floor. With all of the power outages and issues my mom didn't realize that the traffic lights were not working correctly. She had a green light but so did everyone else because the lights weren't working. Traffic was extremely heavy and somebody pulled out in front of us and my mom hit them. I came off the front seat and my head hit the dashboard and my fishbowl tipped over. I was crying because I was scared and probably hurt and then when I realized my fish tipped over I cried even harder. I was more concerned with my fish being okay than I was with anything else. I probably didn't even realize what was going on, I was three. I remember sitting in the back of the ambulance and they were checking my eyes to see if anything was wrong or if I had a concussion. I just kept asking about my fish. That was all I cared about, continually asking if my fish was okay. Eventually, an EMS worker came up to me with my fish in the fishbowl letting me know that it was okay. I was so very happy that my fish was okay. I asked the EMS guy to check out my fish as well. I remember them being very thorough but I'm sure that they just did what they needed to do to appease a three-year-old, and it worked. I think about where God was when this happened. I was three sitting in the front seat of a car, with no seatbelt. Seatbelts weren't even a required law until July of

1985 (so I'm told) so I know that He was right there with me holding my hand, and I believe that He was protecting my fish as well. It amazes me that I still have this memory from when I was three years old. God knew I would remember this. He knew that I would reflect on where he was when all of this happened. He loves me so much. God cares about the little things so think about how much more he cares about the big things that happened in our lives. That has to be a refreshing thought, it has to give you hope and a promise. If it doesn't, then you don't know the heart of God. You must know that he loves you more than anything.

Matthew 6:26 says "Look at the birds of the air: they neither sow nor reap nor gather into barns, and yet your heavenly Father feeds them. Are you not of more value than they?"

Read and Journal.
Day 1: Matthew 6:25-34
Day 2: 1 Peter 5:7
Day 3: Matthew 6:30
Day 4: Psalm 55:22
Day 5: 1 John 4:9-10
Day 6: Isaiah 46:4
Day 7: Romans 6:23

Write down one thing each day that you are thankful for.

Week 4: Grandpa & Grandma's House

Have you ever been to those places in your life, in those moments where you just feel so safe and secure? Like nothing can hurt you, harm you, or even make your day bad? I always felt that way when going to my grandparents' home in Berkley, Michigan. I remember going over to their home to visit, and my grandmother would always make me tea and have windmill cookies. There was a baby doll that sat on her stairs that led to the upstairs bedroom that was once my father's as a child. I would play with that doll like it was my own. I have a porcelain piggy bank that my grandma gave me. It's beautiful and has flowers on it and is full of pennies. A stuffed brown bunny that she gave me when I was 5 still sits on my dresser after all these years. There was a large mirror that hung on the wall just above their couch. I loved that mirror. It's old and has an old-fashioned frame around it. There were all kinds of Dutch knick knacks in her home, and she would teach me all about them. She would talk to me about being Dutch and what the Dutch people did and how they lived. At Christmas time there would be ribbon candy and the house would smell of whatever wonderful things were cooking in the oven. The entire family would come over and we would spend time together that formed memories that I will never forget. We would open gifts, share stories, and laugh. I remember always wanting to sit on my grandmother's lap. She had kind eyes and a beautiful smile. It made you feel warm, safe, and welcomed. There's just something about my grandparents that made you feel so safe and secure. They were a lot like Jesus. I just loved everything about going there. As I think about my grandma and grandpa, I can't help but think that is how Jesus wants us to feel about Him. That He is safe and there's nothing to

14

fear because He's with you. In August of 1979, my grandmother passed away. I was only 6 years old, but I remember times with her fondly. I remember feeling very sad when she passed away. Something was gone from my life. At 6 years old I had to try to understand why. This was the first time I experienced someone passing away and leaving the earth forever. I vividly remember not crying but feeling sad. It was like a switch was turned off and she was never coming back. My grandpa was an amazing man, and I valued all the time I was able to spend with my grandpa after grandma went home to be with Jesus. Time is precious, and I wanted to make the most of those moments. My grandpa passed away in April of 1998. That old mirror I mentioned now sits above my couch, and I think of them every day. Thank you, Grandma and Grandpa, for making your home safe and secure.

I'm so very thankful that I have the Lord in my life. I don't ever have to feel alone, scared, or unsure. He is always with us. He is our safe haven, our constant. I can't imagine a day in my life not living for the Lord or having the truth. I'm so very thankful that somebody told me about Him and did not withhold it from me. It is our purpose to tell others about Him and to not withhold the truth from those that do not know. Just like my grandmother would tell me everything there was to know about being Dutch, we need to tell others everything there is to know about being a Christian and about the man who died for them because He loves them so much. One day when I get to heaven, I will see her again. Until then, I will continue to show love and truth to those I come in contact with.

Read and Journal.
Day 1: Deuteronomy 31:6
Day 2: Isaiah 41:10
Day 3: Proverbs 2:11
Day 4: Psalms 5:11
Day 5: Psalms 12:5
Day 6: Psalms 20:1
Day 7: Psalms 46:1
Write down one thing each day that you are thankful for.

Week 5: Hope: What Does it Mean?

Hope is the feeling that what is wanted will turn out for the best. That's why people say, "I hope that happens", "I hope this comes true" or "hope for the best." But the question is, do you walk in hope? Do you ever really think about it? Have you ever really sat down and thought about what you may be hopeful for? The Bible is full of encouraging scriptures to help us stand on hope.

"Being confident of this, that he who began a good work in you will carry it on to completion until the day of Christ Jesus." - Philippians 1:16

I met Jesus when I was a little girl going to a small Baptist Church in Michigan. The bus would come and pick us up probably on a Wednesday to go to church. While the other kids were in youth group, kids my age were in a class called Awanas Club, I was in Sparks which was kindergarten through second grade. We would learn about Jesus, memorize scripture, and get badges when we accomplish scripture. In this class is where I memorized John 3:16 "For God so loved the world that he gave his only son that whoever believes in him shall not perish but have eternal life." This moment in time is when my journey with Hope started. I was about seven years old when God became real to me. Hope entered my heart as a child and I asked him to come into my life and live in my heart. I remember telling my mom that it must be crowded in my heart now that Jesus lives there. I vividly remember thinking that anything was possible because I had Jesus on my side. Somewhere along the way, we stopped going to church which means I stopped going to Awanas and I stopped learning about Jesus. Slowly as I got older, other things started speaking into my life, things that were not positive for me. Years later as a teenager I was experimenting with drugs, drinking, stealing, cussing, having sex, and the list goes on. Would my life have been different if we stayed in church? Maybe? I don't blame my parents and I've never really thought about blaming them, it was just something that happened. I still believed in Jesus, I even still had hope. I remember praying when I needed something. I rededicated my life when I was 18. Jesus was with me the whole time, patiently waiting on me. My hope never faded while I was in the fire of life. Jesus never gave up hope for me and so why would I give up hope that he could restore my life? At 18, I opened my heart back up to the Lord, all that I knew was restored, and in the years to follow the Lord continued to pour into me. My hope is in him, then, now and always. He is my strength. He is my rock. He is my truth. He who began a good work in me will carry it through! My hope!!

"Being confident of this, that he who began a good work in you will carry it on to completion until the day of Christ Jesus." - Philippians 1:16

Read and Journal
Day 1: 1 Peter 5:10
Day 2: Deuteronomy 3:16
Day 3: Galatians 6:10
Day 4: Hebrews 11:11
Day 5: Isaiah 40:31
Day 6: Jeremiah 29:11
Day 7: Colossians 1:27

Write down one thing each day that you are thankful for.

Week 6: What Did I Just See?

It was the summer of 1980. I was 7 years old. I lived in the country and didn't have many friends that lived close by. The one friend I did have who lived close by was grounded. So I needed to figure out something to do so I wasn't so bored. Next door to our driveway there was an old barn; I speak about this barn in other devotionals in this book. We moved to this house in Swartz Creek, Michigan when I was 3, and this barn had been here since I can remember. I'm sure this barn has lots of memories- I know it has memories for me, and I can imagine the memories it has for other people as well. Unfortunately, the stories that I am telling you about this barn are not necessarily good memories. There's the barn fight, there's the time I watched the barn burn down which obviously happened later, and then there's this story. My parents have lived in that house for 45 years. Over those 45 years, several people have bought and sold the house next door that this barn belonged to. So the people who owned the house and the barn in this story had horses, sheep, goats, pigs, and chickens. I guess you'd say they were farmers. As far as I remember, the husband and wife hired farmhands and they had a nanny who helped with the children. I was outside playing and I went down to the barn to feed the horses and pet the cats. I went running down the hill and ran right into the barn, and that's when I saw it. I saw a man and a woman kissing; however, the man was kissing a woman who was not his wife. It was the nanny. I know this sounds like a movie but it was my real life. I was in shock for just a moment, and luckily for me, as fast as I ran into that barn I was able to turn around and run as fast as I could back home. I have no idea if they saw me or even knew that I was there, and I didn't stop to look back to see if they did. I am so glad that the Lord was with me during this.

He made sure that I ran and I didn't freeze and stand there staring. That would have been very bad.

I ran to the house and I told my mom that I needed to tell her something, and I told her the entire story of what just happened. For some reason, I thought I was going to be in trouble for what I just saw. Sometimes you just can't unsee things. I am also very thankful that I told my mom right away. I know a lot of kids keep things to themselves because they are afraid, so they stay silent. To this day I still have that memory and that visual of what I saw. This was also the start of a query of questions for my mom. Isn't he married? Doesn't the nanny know he's married? Why would he do that? Does the wife know? What about the kids? Are you going to call and tell his wife what I just saw? Do we pretend this never happened? I remember my mom telling me that it wasn't my concern and not to worry about it. That was the end of that conversion, my mom and I never talked about it after that. I don't know if she ever talked to the neighbor, but I do know that they ended up getting divorced within the year.

There are always consequences for our actions. In this case, it was divorce. I don't know what happened to them, I was a child, but I have prayed that they both have found God and are living in joy. At 7 years old I didn't understand that fully. I definitely didn't understand it from a spiritual aspect. Our choices and what we do not only affect ourselves but it affects the future and the people around us. The wages of sin is death, right?

"For the wages of sin is death, but the gift of God is eternal life." - Romans 6:23

Read and Journal
Day 1: Galatians 6:7
Day 2: James 2:10
Day 3: 2 Peter 3:9
Day 4: Jeremiah 17:9-10
Day 5: Romans 13:4
Day 6: Deuteronomy 28:1-68

Day 7: Proverbs 25:2

Write down one thing each day that you are thankful for.

Week 7: Burn, Barn, Burn.

Here we go again- another barn story. As much as this barn seemed to hold a lot of secrets and bad memories, I loved playing in it. I was a kid and I didn't really understand all the secrets it held. That was all about to end. The year was 1982; I was 9. The neighbor girl and I were in my garage. My mom had boxes and boxes full of old magazines, I called them "mom magazines". Ever heard of Family Circle or Better Homes and Gardens? There were many others, as well. We were looking at houses and talking about what we would want our home to look like, what our gardens would grow, and what kind of flowers our flowerbeds would have. Normal girl stuff, right? All of a sudden, I heard my mom screaming my name. She had gone to pick my brother up from driver's training and wasn't home when we went into the garage. I heard her screaming and we ran out of the garage to see the barn that sat about 200 feet from our driveway ablaze with smoke and fire. It took my breath away. I had never seen anything like it. Then I heard the fire trucks. It was in that moment that my mom hugged me, crying. I didn't understand why she was crying- it's just a barn and it's not even ours. That's how a 9-year-old mind seems to work. She wasn't crying because of the barn I soon learned. She thought I was in that barn since I played so often in it. It took me many years to understand that mother's love. When you think you are losing your child, the sorrow and helplessness is overwhelming. We later found out that the barn burned down because my neighbor's brother hid adult magazines and cigarettes in there. A cigarette burned that barn down. In all reality, sin burned that barn to the ground. All the animals got out and no one was hurt, thankfully. I missed walking out of the house and seeing the barn. You may be wondering what this has to do with God and how it applies in a devotional. God's hand kept us away from the barn that day. We played in that barn practically every day. That's why my mom thought that I was inside. We never hung out in my garage. I never played in there, but this day we did. By God's grace we did. God is in every situation you are in. Good or bad, He is there. No matter the outcome, He is there. He doesn't create bad things or situation, but He uses them to teach and makes all things beautiful if we let him. Maybe I didn't play in the barn that day and escaped the fire and experienced every other story you have read and will read simply to write this book to hopefully change someone's life, encourage someone, to remind someone that they are worth it. Not because I say so, but because He says so!

"But let all who take refuge in you be glad; let them ever sing for joy. Spread your protection over them, that those who love your name may rejoice in you." Psalms 5:11

Let's take this week and dig into God's protection over us.

1. Have you ever been in a situation from which you were saved?
2. If so, what was it? How did God protect you?
3. Have you ever been somewhere you weren't supposed to be and something bad happened?
4. If so, what happened and how did God protect you?
5. Pray for someone who needs God's protection. Continue to pray for them for the rest of the week.

Read and Journal

Day 1: 2 Thessalonians 3:3
Day 2: Deuteronomy 31:6
Day 3: Isaiah 41:10
Day 4: Proverbs 2:11
Day 5: Proverbs 4:6
Day 6: Psalm 20:1
Day 7: Psalm 34:19

Write down one thing each day that you are thankful for.

Week 8: Feeling Shame When It's Not Your Fault.

It took me quite some time to come up with the title of this devotional. As you know, all of these are stories of my life. This one is a little harder to talk about than others. When I was younger, I believe around seven or eight, I was molested. Not just once, not twice, but three times. Three times by three different people within several years of each other. The first time it happened I was at a neighbor's house playing outside in the yard. It was about the time of year when people were going camping. So they had their tent set up to air it out. An older boy came over. I didn't think anything of it- he was a friend of my brother's. He and a friend of his were in the tent just relaxing, and they had chocolate bars. I remember him offering me some chocolate but telling me I had to come into the tent in order to get some. Knowing what I know now, I would never have done that; however, I was a child, and I was trusting. I went into the tent to get the chocolate and before I got the chocolate he zipped up the tent. I won't go into detail about what happened, but I will simply say that what happened to me changed my life. I didn't make a sound. I was terrified, petrified- I literally couldn't move and I didn't know what to do. I was never taught what to do in this kind of situation, so I didn't have a reaction to what was happening. After about what felt like forever, he left the tent and I just sat there and cried. The friend whose house I was at came into the tent and asked what was wrong, and I told him. He ran into his house to tell his mom. I was thinking that if he told his mom it would be a good thing, because a mother is supposed to protect you right? Well, I was told that I was naughty, wrong, and bad. I was told to sit in a chair, next to the garbage can in a dirty, stinky garage to think about what I did. *What did I do wrong?*

23

Am I dirty and bad because I allowed this to happen? I didn't say no, so this must be my fault! All of these thoughts were going through my mind. After about what felt like an hour, which was probably only like 10 minutes, I got up, left the garage, and ran home. I don't believe that she told my mom because when I got home my mom didn't say anything to me. I never told my mom what happened until I was an adult and married with my own children.

The second time it happened, I was over at a girlfriend's house, and we were playing hide and seek with the neighbor boys in the woods. I was hiding and one of the older boys found me. He grabbed me from behind, put his hand over my mouth, and told me not to scream then proceeded to inappropriately touch me through my clothes. I once again "allowed" it to happen. I never screamed and I never said no. I never told anyone what happened because the first time I told someone, I was told I was wrong and that it was my fault. I never told my parents about this incident.

The third time it happened hit a little closer to home because it was a family member. It was less invasive than the others but still a violation. I told my mother, and as far as I know, she dealt with it. I say that because I didn't witness her talking to the person and it was never brought up again. For years and years, I held onto what had happened to me. For a very long time, I thought the only thing I was good for was what I could use my body for. So that's what I did to get what I wanted. It wasn't until I began a relationship with Jesus that I found my identity and I was able to forgive myself and walk in true freedom. I was literally set free by scripture. Reading over and over again what God says about me and who He says I am and believing it. Once I got to this point, I was able to find forgiveness for those who had wronged me. I later learned that the boy from the first incident came from an abusive home with an alcoholic father who abused him. It doesn't make what he did right, but it made it more understandable. I felt sadness for him. He later passed away from an overdose. I read in the paper years later as an adult that the boy from the second incident had passed away in a car accident. I never had a chance to forgive him while he was alive, but I had forgiven him all the same. The third person was a little harder to forgive because it was a little closer to home, but I did find forgiveness because none of us are perfect and we all make mistakes, especially when we are young. I even wrote him a letter as an adult apologizing for our lack of relationship and wanting to restore something that was lost. He read it and never responded to it, and that's okay. I am free from shame, and I've set him free by forgiving him. I was very promiscuous as a teen but God has restored me. He alone has made me pure and precious. All of this is a direct result of poor choices on behalf of other people. I was just in the wrong place at the wrong time, but even during that, God was with me the entire time. He never turned away from me or left me alone. I walked in shame for so many years for something that wasn't my doing or my fault. Through this I found my voice and my identity. It may have come years later, but it came, nonetheless.

"Therefore, there is now no condemnation for those who are in Christ Jesus." Romans 8:1

"For in Christ all the fullness of the Deity lives in bodily form, and in Christ you have been brought to fullness. He is the head over every power and authority." Colossians 2:9-10

1. Do you feel guilty for something that isn't your fault?
If so, what is it?
2. Do you know now that it isn't your fault? It's not your fault!!
3. Are there things in your life you need to let go of? People you need to forgive? If so, write down their names and begin to forgive them.
4. Take this time to remind yourself what and who God says you are.
5. Think of that friend or family member that needs freedom from guilt that isn't theirs to carry and pray for them. Send them an encouraging text or call.

Read and Journal. These scriptures are just to remind you who you are in Christ.
Day 1: Jeremiah 1:5
Day 2: 1 Peter 2:9
Day 3: John 1:12

Day 4: Romans 8:17
Day 5: 2 Corinthians 5:17
Day 6: Psalms 139:14
Day 7: Ephesians 5:8

Write down one thing each day that you are thankful for.

Week 9: The Barn Fight

Ever been in the wrong place at the wrong time? I feel like I have a lot of those kinds of stories, and I probably should start many of these devotionals with that very sentence. I don't know if it's just me or kids in general, but here is another story of being at the wrong place at the wrong time. There used to be a very large barn that sat next to my parents' driveway in my neighbor's yard. They had horses, chickens, and barn cats. I would go in there all the time and play, petting and feeding the horses and chasing the cats. Normal kid stuff. One time, the girl next door and my friend from down the street were in there playing. The girl whose barn we were in had a great idea and thought it would be funny if myself and my friend would fight each other. I remember her saying we could only stay and play if we fought each other. Like she literally wanted us to punch each other in the face. At first, I thought she was joking, and so did my friend. I was about 13 at this time. I had never been in a fight in my entire life, and I didn't want to start now. I asked her why she wanted us to do that and if she was joking, and in the middle of me asking the question my friend decided to go ahead with her idea. She pushed me, hard, and I fell in horse manure.

Let me back the story up a little bit. My older brother and I don't have the greatest relationship; we never really did, but this particular day he let me wear one of his button-up cowboy shirts. It was blue and had white pearly buttons and red roses on it. It was big on me but I loved it. So when I realized that there was now horse manure on the shirt that I begged him to wear and I knew he was going to be very mad at me, something snapped. I didn't know that I had such rage inside of me. I got up and with both of my hands, I reached up to each side of her head, grabbed her ear lobes, and ripped out her earrings. It was pretty bloody, and there was crying, screaming, and gnashing of teeth, or so it seemed. My friend was crying and the girl that suggested it was laughing. I wanted so badly to punch the girl who antagonized it all, but it was at this moment that I knew that I was in a lot of trouble. So I had a choice to make and I needed to make it quickly. I ran home and I told my mom that my friend pushed me in horse manure and that I needed her to wash the shirt immediately. Yep, that's what I was concerned with. The fact that there was horse poop on my brother's shirt. It wasn't until my friend's mom called my mom that I realized I probably should have filled her in on the rest of the story and what I did to my friend's earlobes.

Oddly enough we were still friends after this, and there are a few stories in this book that have to do with that friend. I was not a very nice child, and that friend put up with a lot from me. I would like to say that we still talk to this day- not often, but we stay in touch. There are going to be times in your life when you are going to be under such pressure that you need to make a decision in a moment and that decision needs to be the right decision. It's an obvious statement for me to say that my decision to run home and tell my mom to wash the shirt was not the right decision to make. What matters to us most is what we will take care of first. My priority was to make sure that shirt was clean so my brother was not mad. My priority should've been to make sure my friend was okay. To back it up a little further, my priority should've been to not respond to being pushed down into horse manure. It was at that moment that I probably should've walked home.

What does the Bible say about priorities? There are several scriptures about priorities in the Bible.

Romans 12:2 - "Do not be conformed to this world, but be transformed by the renewal of your mind, that by testing you may discern what is the will of God, what is good and acceptable and perfect."

Read and Journal.
Day 1: Matthew 6:33

Day 2: Luke 12:34
Day 3: Exodus 20:3
Day 4: 1 Timothy 3:5
Day 5: Luke 12-22-34
Day 6: Deuteronomy 6:5
Day 7: Luke 10:38-42

Write down one thing each day that you are thankful for.

Week 10: I Think That Was Laced

Have you ever had a friend, a friend that you can't wait to spend every single waking moment with? To seek every adventure, to dance all the new dances, to watch movies, to eat pizza and drink pop with? After a night of adventure and partying and doing things we shouldn't have, we would come home and eat bologna and mustard. That's it, just bologna with mustard. I had that friend and I adored her. I trusted her with everything that I had and she trusted me. We still talk, not often, but we talk and pray for each other from time to time. I remember we were sitting in her room and she told me that she had a joint. It was already rolled and ready to go. I didn't think much of it because we've done this before, but this time it was different. It was laced with coke, but I didn't know that until after we had smoked it. She didn't do it to be mean, and she wasn't trying to hurt me; she just thought it was funny and that it would be fun. I don't know how addicting coke is and I'm thankful for that. I am lucky to say that I did not become addicted to it and I never did it again. I guess I wouldn't use the word lucky- I would say I was blessed and protected by a Father who loved me even when I didn't know it yet. I would say the same for my friend. He's protected her from so many things and I know that she loves the Lord. It's amazing to think of things that we did together and then later in life both of us serving and loving God. This might just seem like a little story and I'm sure people read this and think they've done worse, and maybe you have, but for me it was something that I later realized just another moment that God was there with me protecting me. Was He sitting by just thinking, "Geez, when are these girls gonna get it?" (Probably not, because He knows everything so He knew when it would happen.) He probably sat by just protecting us and keeping us safe. I am thankful for the many, many times that He has protected me throughout all of the poor decision-making of my youth.

As the song says, "It may look like I'm surrounded, but I'm surrounded by you." 1 Corinthians 10:13 says, "No temptation has overtaken you except what is common to mankind. And God is faithful; He will not let you be tempted beyond what you can bear. But when you are tempted, He will also provide a way out so that you can endure it."

Thank you, God, for allowing me to endure the things that I've been tempted by and providing a way out.

Read and Journal.

Day 1: Proverbs 3:5-6
Day 2: Galatians 6:7-8
Day 3: 1 Corinthians 15:33
Day 4: 1 Corinthians 10:13
Day 5: Proverbs 11:14
Day 6: James 1:5
Day 7: Joshua 1:8

Write down one thing each day that you are thankful for.

Week 11: My 16th Birthday. It's Not That Great.

What do you think about when you think about your 16th birthday? I'm not really sure what I thought was going to happen for my 16th birthday. I didn't know if I was going to have a huge surprise party, because, after all, I'm 16! Like that's some kind of special occasion or something. I didn't know if I was going to have my dream car in the driveway with a big bow tied around it or if all my friends would come over and for some reason, my parents would just let me have a party and they would go away. I have no idea what I was thinking, but I thought it was going to be great. I had two friends over for my 16th birthday. There was no big party. There was no car in the driveway with a big bow around it. Honestly, I guess it was pretty lame compared to what my mind was telling me it was going to be. Perspective is everything, right? At the time I didn't know this, but I know it now. I know now that you can make any situation what you want it to be because if you go into things with a good attitude, anything can be fun. Life isn't boring. If your life is boring that means you're boring, and I'm not boring! I don't remember what we did. I don't remember any of the jokes we made or anything like that, but I do have a picture from it and the people I chose to be around the day were my very best friends at the time.

I have learned to be content in all things even when the fantasies in my head make the occasion bigger than it really is. I really don't regret any of the people that I was friends with. They were good people. They were good friends (as good as I they knew how to be at that point in life). I know for sure I could've been a better friend. I still am in contact with many of them. Many of us lead different lives, have families, have grandchildren, and for the most part, we are happy people. They all know my relationship with God, they know what I believe, and they know that at any time they can always call or text me and I will be there for them praying for whatever the situation calls for.

Life is about perspective. Every year we go to Boise, Idaho. In Boise, there's a place called Table Rock. It's about a 45-minute hike up the side of this what I like to call "mountain." I'm sure to the people of Idaho it's more of a small hill. From ground level you can't really see much- the parking lot and what's around you- but as you start walking, the view gets better. You start to see further and wider, and then you walk up more and you see even more of the city, and by the time you get to the top, you can see miles and miles and miles. You can see mountains off into the distance, and it looks like it just borders everything. It's a very hard hike for those who aren't used to hiking, and I think perspective is, too. Perspective is hard for those who don't use it. I think it's important to dissect the situations that we're in and change our perspective of it, to pull out the good in what might seem like a bad situation. Perspective will influence everything you do. It influences our attitudes, our mindset, our viewpoint, our outlook, and our beliefs. Remember to read the scriptures with a Godly perspective.

Read and Journal
Day 1: Psalm 9:7-8
Day 2: Psalm 73:26
Day 3: Psalm 100:5
Day 4: 2 Corinthians 4:17-18
Day 5: 1 Thessalonians 4:17
Day 6: Hebrews 9:12
Day 7: Hebrews 13:8

Write down one thing each day that you are thankful for.

Week 12: Naïve and in a Drug House

It's every parent's nightmare, although I somehow saved my parents from this terrible dream. Yes, I did it, but God protected me from every poor choice I made along the way. Wow, I am so grateful for such a loving, caring, compassionate God! I would be such a wreck if my child did this. I can only imagine His concerns when I was so reckless. When I was about 16, I was dating a guy that I trusted wholeheartedly. He had friends who lived in Flint. I didn't know that I shouldn't have been where I was. My parents always told me to stay away from certain areas in Flint, but I clearly didn't listen. I figured they just didn't want me to have any fun, because isn't that what parents do? Stop their children from having fun? Insert face-palm emoji here. What a silly thought!! As a parent, I now understand it was to keep me safe.

Anyway, we went to his friend's house in Flint, or so I thought. We walked into the home. Dim lighting, very little furniture in the common areas, and no furniture in the bedrooms. Almost everyone that was there was in the kitchen around the table doing coke. There were guns on the counter and in some of the guys' back pockets. There were a few people in the bedrooms laid out on the floor- passed out. People would come and go every so often and that's when it dawned on me. I have single-handedly found myself in a drug house. Now I'm starting to panic. I stayed with my friend the whole time we were there. I didn't know why we were even there, but I quickly figured it out. He was buying drugs. At this point in my life, I'm no angel and the substances I used up to this point were given to me by people I knew and trusted. I had never seen it go down like this. I was a bit intimidated. Thankfully, we didn't stay too long- he did what he needed to do and we left. I never asked him how he knew them, what he bought, or why in the world he took me with him. I just remember thinking, "Wow, that could have been bad in so many different ways." There could have been a drug raid, and being in the wrong place at the wrong time I could have gotten in a lot of trouble. I could have easily been abused or raped. I don't mean to sound so dramatic, but really, what the heck?? I could have gotten hurt in so many different ways. However, I wasn't. I was protected. Not by the friend I was with physically but by God, supernatural. He protected me. He always has through every thoughtless choice I have ever made.

His love reminds me of the song Reckless Love.

Before I spoke a word, You were singing over me
You have been so, so good to me
Before I took a breath, You breathed Your life in me. You have been so, so kind to me
Oh, the overwhelming, never-ending, reckless love of God
Oh, it chases me down, fights 'til I'm found, leaves the ninety-nine
I couldn't earn it, and I don't deserve it, still, You give Yourself away
Oh, the overwhelming, never-ending, reckless love of God, yeah
There's no shadow You won't light up
Mountain You won't climb up
Coming after me
There's no wall You won't kick down
Lie You won't tear down
Coming after me
He LOVES me!!!

John 3:16- "For God so loved the world, that he gave his only begotten Son, that whosoever believeth in him shall not perish, but have everlasting life."

Read and Journal

Day 1: 1 Corinthians 13:13
Day 2: 1 John 3:1
Day 3: 1 John 4:7
Day 4: 1 John 4:8

Day 5: 1 John 4:16
Day 6: 1 John 4:18
Day 7: 1 John 4:19

Write down one thing each day that you are thankful for.

Week 13: So I Dated a Satanist

This is about God's hand on my life and the protection he has always had on me. When I was about 16, I met a guy through a friend. He was actually my best friend's boyfriend's friend. Let me tell you a little about 16-year-old me. Appearance-wise, I was tall, thin, and beautiful. I didn't think that about myself then, but looking back, I see it. I see my daughters as I look at old pictures of me and I think they are gorgeous so I must have been OK. I was naive- extremely naive. I took a lot of chances because I didn't completely think through situations, like ever. I knew choices had consequences, but I never took the time to think about what those consequences would be. I wasn't stupid, but I was ignorant of my choices. He was a tall, attractive, blonde boy. He was quiet, and only really talked when he had something to say. He was friendly, kind, and loyal. What could go wrong?

I went to his house once; he lived about 20 minutes from me. We were meeting friends at his house then we were going to the mall. That's what we did for fun 30 years ago. This was the first time meeting his mom. She was welcoming and she had a warm smile. The kind that makes you feel safe. She invited me in and showed me around. I felt comfortable. Now up to this point in our relationship, I had never felt awkward or nervous around him. He asked me to come to his room so we could hang out. Let me fill you in a little. This guy had never even held my hand, tried to kiss me, or anything like that, so I wasn't afraid to go with him. I wasn't nervous until I stepped foot into his room. The atmosphere changed. It was an eerie feeling, a feeling I had never felt before. My chest felt tight and everything around me was dark. It was not physically dark- the sun was shining bright through his windows- but there was something dark in his room. It's what I had imagined evil to feel like. He had weird drawings and pictures on his walls. Strange symbols were written everywhere. There was a skull on his dresser and a stuffed crow.

It was definitely different for me. His mannerisms seemed the same, so I started asking him about what I was seeing. He began to tell me that he was a warlock and that he practiced Satanic spells. That he read the satanic bible and followed what it said. Honestly, I wanted to laugh. What kind of junk is he trying to tell me right now? I thought it was a joke at first then I thought about the way his room looked and to top it off he gave me a satanic bible of my own. Wow!! How nice of him? I took it but by this time I was a little creeped out. He was confusing me for sure. He was so kind but what he was into was so dark. He was saying things like "We will be together forever," and "I'll never leave you and you will never leave me." He said we could do spells and sacrifices together. It was like some kind of show- like it wasn't real. *Sabrina the Teenage Witch* gone bad. I felt very uncomfortable by this time and just wanted to leave. I asked him if we could go downstairs and wait for our friends. I don't know if he knew I was uncomfortable and I didn't care, I just wanted to leave. I wondered if his mom knew what he was into. How do I break up with this guy? I was now a little scared of him but at the same time, I think it's all ridiculous. I believed in God. I didn't have a relationship with God at this point in my life, but I believed He was real. I know now that God was protecting me from this boy who came off so kind and gentle.

He decided not to go with us to the mall that day. I'm not sure why. As I was getting ready to leave with my friends he took my hand and gave me $70. He said, "This is for you; I need you to keep this for me." That's all he said. I agreed politely but I wasn't thinking nice things. I didn't even question him as to why. I knew I was breaking up with him and I didn't want to see him again, but I was scared to tell him at this point, so I left with his money and Satanic bible. What a weird sentence that is. Sometimes I think of the things I did and think, "How is this real?" So I told my friends all about what I saw and how strange it was. This was their advice to me. Break up with him and spend his money. OK, sounds doable!! The person I am today would never do that but the person I was then did. I spent it, broke up with him, and told him I didn't want to talk to him ever again. I feel like maybe that was a bit dramatic, but at 16 things tend to be theatrical.

He called me one day and asked for his money, and my friend jumped into the conversation and let him know we spent it and to leave me alone. (That was the clean version of what was said). He was silent on the other end of the phone and simply hung up. A few weeks later my friends and I were at the mall, and I hadn't heard from him at all. We were going up the escalator and I saw him sitting in a chair. We made eye contact and he mouthed, "I'm going to kill you." I just froze, looking at him and he mouthed it again. I turned around and told my friend what he said. She proceeded to yell very loudly for what felt like a few hundred people to hear with some colorful choice words on my behalf. And that was it. He didn't follow us or anything. It was over. I did talk to him once after this on the phone, I apologized for spending his money. He calmly said, "It's okay," and hung up. That's the last I ever heard from him.

You may be wondering what happened to the satanic bible he gave me. I read a chapter or two. It was creepy and demonic. Complete opposite of what God's word says. I was going to rip it up, possibly even burn it. I took it to school; I don't know why. I think I felt like a rebel with it even though I thought it was stupid. My peers were already scared of me so why not give them one more reason to avoid me? I gave it to my principal, told him an ex-boyfriend gave it to me and I didn't want it anymore. He told me he would throw it away for me and to stay away from boys, every boy, forever.

This could have been worse. Much worse. The enemy is smart. He wanted me to get involved with the occult, but God is smarter. I had discernment even before I knew what it was. I knew to run from this. I thank God for protecting me and keeping me safe. I pray for this guy; I pray that somewhere along the way, God captured his heart.

"Above all else, guard your heart, for everything you do flows from it." - Proverbs 4:23

"Do not forsake wisdom, and she will protect you; love her, and she will watch over you. The beginning of wisdom is this: Get wisdom. Though it cost all you have, get understanding." - Proverbs 4:6-7

Read and Journal
Day 1: 1 Corinthians 10:13
Day 2: 2 Thessalonians 3:3
Day 3: Deuteronomy 31:6
Day 4: Isaiah 41:10
Day 5: Proverbs 2:11
Day 6: Psalm 5:11
Day 7: Psalm 34:19

Write down one thing each day that you are thankful for.

Week 14: My Neighbor Killed Someone

What does it look like when we assume things, good or bad? What if I told you that my neighbor killed someone? This devotional is less funny and/or entertaining than the other ones may have been and more on the serious side. I'm leaving names out to protect those families involved. I had a neighbor that I went to school with from kindergarten through high school. He was quiet, kept to himself, he was kind and gentle, and was a bit on the "nerdy" side if we are stereotyping, and apparently, I am. Up to that point in my life, I'd never known him to be violent, mean, or angry. He never showed typical signs of abuse, depression, or anger. I don't know the details of his home life but because of what he did I could make assumptions and probably fill in the blanks, but I won't do that either. I don't know what happened in his home behind closed doors. Just like we don't know what people are going through or dealing with on a daily basis. We can guess, speculate, and pass judgments, but we don't know unless they tell us. I guarantee that if the right person knew what he was going through, they would have gotten him help or told the right authorities. Sometimes, we hide behind a mask so no one knows what we are truly dealing with.

My husband and I were youth pastors for over 18 years, and I am thankful that I put in the time to get a certificate in counseling. It has helped put parents at ease. There is something about a framed certification on the wall in your office that eases the parent's mind that you "know what you are doing." I am not sure we ever know what we are doing, but I do know that my trust is in the Lord and He knows what He is doing. This assumption that the certificate on the wall made me wiser simply isn't true. I gave the same advice before I had a certificate on the wall, and it was all biblically based and always pointed back to Jesus. There have been many times that I have had to talk to a parent, guardian, or the police about situations that a student confided in me about. Things that were deeper than a prayer and a hug, situations that needed to be dealt with because it wasn't safe for the student to return home. Sometimes people get upset or say they will be mad if you tell someone. That's fear talking. Somewhere deep within they know that it's for their safety in the long run that someone is told what is going on.

I wish the classmate that I went to school with knew that. I wish he had someone he could have talked to, and I wish if he was talking to someone that they would have told someone. Even if he would have been "mad" in the moment. The world calls that "snitching," and as the saying goes, "snitches end up in ditches." The truth is that the person needing to be "snitched" on needs help themselves. The truth sets us free. The boy I went to school with killed his mom and stepdad with a shotgun as they slept in their bed and then he and his younger brother came to school like it was a normal day. Was he protecting his younger brother from something? Was he protecting himself? Was he simply mad? We can assume all day long. I remember the police showing up and hearing he was escorted out of the school. Rumors flew all over the school that day, that week that was all anyone talked about and eventually it died down and something else would be the talk of the time. I don't know what happened to him after that. I can guess but that's assuming, isn't it?

I don't know where he is today or if he knows the love of the Lord, but I pray for him and I pray that he does or gets an opportunity to know Him. Let's talk about speaking the truth. We don't know what people are dealing with in their lives. It doesn't matter what people show you on the outside- it doesn't make it true. Most of what we see on Facebook and Instagram is staged, and they are only showing us what they want us to see. You don't know about the drunken fight that happened after that beautiful picture of their vacation was posted. We don't know about the drug addiction that goes along with the post of the raise they got at work. We don't know about the abuse that he or she endures, we just see the picture that is posted of a big smile and some witty quote. Take into consideration that everyone has a story, a past, a testimony but they are only showing us what they want us to know. I try to remember that when meeting people. We all have a story. We all are sorting through things in our lives. Let's be there for one another and let's not be so quick to judge. We don't know what we would do until we are their shoes. Assuming reveals more about what's in our heart than it does about the other person.

Philippians 2:4 - "Don't be concerned only about your own interests, but also be concerned about the interests of others."

Matthew 7:1 - "Judge not, that you be not judged."

7 scriptures where assuming something plays a part. Read and Journal.
Day 1: Joshua 14:12
Day 2: 1 Chronicles 28:7
Day 3: 1 Chronicles 28:9
Day 4: Proverbs 31:16
Day 5: Matthew 9:30
Day 6: Matthew 24:5
Day 7: Mark 13:6

Write down one thing a day you are thankful for.

Week 15: And Then it Snowed Glitter

Even before I knew the Lord, He protected and watched over me. Why I was protected to the extent that I was will remain a mystery until I sit at His feet on the day I go home to be with Him. Until then, I will continue to thank Him each and every time I am reminded how He saved me from situations I put myself in. I started experimenting with drugs and alcohol at a young age. When I was 11 and in 6th grade, I started smoking marijuana, smoking basically anything we could get our hands on, drinking alcohol, and taking chances with different drugs. I honestly don't know how I wasn't addicted except by God's grace. I found myself in many compromising situations. The day I stopped playing around with drugs was life-changing. From a young age, I knew God was real, so I knew I could always call on Him. I just didn't have a relationship with Him yet.

When I was 17, I used to stay the weekends at a friend's house with her and her husband. They got married very young- she was 17 and he was 19. I would stay every weekend with them and party. It was August of 1990. We spent the evening drinking and smoking and somehow decided it would be a good idea to do some acid. I'd done this a few times prior to this so I wasn't worried. It got late and I was getting tired, so I wanted to try to sleep. I went into the room I was staying in and lay down. I was staring at the ceiling which was a glittery popcorn ceiling. If you don't know what that looks like, Google it. Suddenly, it started snowing glitter. It was falling from the ceiling, and it was beautiful. I looked down at the floor, and it was building up like snow does. I could touch it and throw it. It continued to pile up and I realized it was starting to cover me. The reality that this wasn't real hit me, but I could still see all the glitter. This drug sends you into a hallucinating state. So, this is what I was experiencing. It kept getting deeper and deeper. It was almost covering my entire body.

That's when it happened. I started to panic and hyperventilate. I said "God, I know this isn't real. Please allow me to go to sleep and I will never touch a drug again." That's all I said, and that's what He did. I instantly fell asleep. I literally never touched another drug after this. This experience truly changed me. I knew it was God who saved me from freaking out, from a panic attack, or from anything else the enemy was trying to do. This story has always been funny to people because I love glitz and glitter, so the enemy knew what to use. By no means was it funny or fun for me. But time after time, God has had His hands on me. He's always there for us. No matter what it is you are going through, He's right there with you. Even when you willingly make a poor choice. God's word says, "Keep your lives free from the love of money and be content with what you have, because God has said, 'Never will I leave you; never will I forsake you.'" Hebrews 13:5 NIV

Be content with your life- He will never leave you! It then continues and says, "So we say with confidence, 'The Lord is my helper; I will not be afraid. What can mere mortals do to me?'" Hebrews 13:6 NIV

"Be strong and courageous. Do not be afraid or terrified because of them, for the Lord your God goes with you; he will never leave you nor forsake you." Deuteronomy 31:6 NIV

He will never leave you nor forsake you!

1. Do you trust God to protect you? If not, why?
2. If so, write about a time in your life when God protected you.
3. What things come to mind when you think about the protection of God?
4. What things can we do on a daily basis to cover ourselves in God's protection?
5. Say a prayer for someone who could use God's protection in their life.

Read and Journal.
Day 1: Deuteronomy 31:8
Day 2: Joshua 1:5
Day 3: Joshua 1:9
Day 4: Isaiah 41:10
Day 5: Deuteronomy 4:31
Day 6: Matthew 28:20
Day 7: Psalms 118:6

Write down one thing each day that you are thankful for.

Week 16: Capitol Theater, Flint Town

In the early 1990s, my friends and I used to go to punk and rock shows at the Capitol Theater. It was October of 1990 and we went to see Danzig. In order to go to these shows, I had to lie to my parents about what I was doing and where I was. At this time, my parents didn't allow me to hang out in Flint. Not only were my parents uneasy about the friends I chose to hang out with, they weren't too happy about the music I chose to listen to, either. I personally didn't listen to a lot of punk music, but the friends I was hanging around at the time did. At this time in my life, I had a friend named Mike who claimed to be a Hare Krishna. Now I didn't know anything about this at this time in my young life, and I really don't know much about it now, but I know that has to do with a Hindu god. Mike was very kind, soft-spoken, and gentle. There's more about him in a different devotional, but let me get back to the Capitol Theater.

I would go to the shows and hang out in Flint because it was what my friends were doing and I would have to lie in order to do it. The music I was listening to was not good for my spirit but at this time in my life, I didn't understand that. This was just before Jesus captured my heart. Nothing crazy or out of the ordinary happens in this experience from my past except for the fact that I lied, I was deceitful to my parents, I was damaging my spirit, and I had no idea. The show went well, I got home on time, and I didn't hurt anyone (or so it seemed) but in the long run, the little lies or even big lies are hurtful, even if you don't get caught. "Catch for us the foxes, the little foxes that ruin the vineyards, our vineyards that are in bloom." - Song of Solomon 2:15 So where do the little foxes come in? The "little foxes" are our sins. Sins of our heart like David had, sins of our lips, sins of our undisciplined tongue, sins in our behavior. Jesus is the vine!!

"I am the true vine, and my Father is the gardener."   - John 15:1

"We as believers are the branches. I am the vine; you are the branches. If you remain in me and I in you, you will bear much fruit; apart from me you can do nothing." - John 15:5

"As branches, we are to bear fruit but if we are away from God we do not bear fruit. If you do not remain in me, you are like a branch that is thrown away and withers; such branches are picked up, thrown into the fire, and burned. If you remain in me and my words remain in you, ask whatever you wish, and it will be done for you. This is to my Father's glory, that you bear much fruit, showing yourselves to be my disciples." -John 15:6-8

"But the fruit of the Spirit is love, joy, peace, forbearance, kindness, goodness, faithfulness, gentleness and self-control. Against such things there is no law." - Galatians 5:22-23

So what does that mean and what does it have to do with this testimony? Even though everything turned out great that night on the outside, on the inside, little foxes were gnawing at my spirit. How do you stop the little foxes? Only the Holy Spirit can do that, which means we must be in the Word and we must be following the Word.

Here are lies Satan tries to tell us…

1. Accountability: There is no reason to tell others what you're going through. James 5:16 - Why is this scripture so important in our daily life?
2. Anger: If I don't do something about it, they will get away with it. Romans 12:19 - Why is this scripture so important in our daily life?
3. Reading the word: It's not that big of a deal. John 8:31 - Why is this scripture so important in our daily life?
4. Forgiveness: I will never forgive what they did to me. Matthew 6:14-15 - Why is this scripture so important in our daily life?
5. Prayer: prayer doesn't work and God doesn't care. Jeremiah 29:13 - Why is this scripture so important in our daily life?

There are so many more lies the enemy tries to tell us. Those were just a few.

Read and Journal
Day 1:John 15:1-2
Day 2: John 15:3-4
Day 3: John 15:5
Day 4: John 15:6
Day 5: John 15:7-8
Day 6: John 15:9-10
Day 7: Song of Solomon 2:15

Write down one thing each day that you are thankful for.

Week 17: Gas Station Potty Mouth

When I was younger, just like many kids, we hung out with other kids who may not have been the best influence. I would probably say that I wasn't the best influence on people. To be completely honest, rather than saying I probably wasn't, I will say I definitely wasn't. There was a time in my life when every other word was a cuss word unless I was around adults or teachers or people of authority. So probably from around 6th grade all the way until I was about 18 my mouth wasn't the greatest thing to hear from. I knew that talking that way was wrong, but I didn't feel convicted by it. The reasoning is that I didn't know the Lord at this time yet. There's something about an understanding of who God is in your life that changes the way that you speak, act, and respond to things. Not knowing him and talking the way that I talked, there was no conviction at this time.

So here's a quick story. I was about 17, and I was in a gas station with some friends grabbing some snacks, Mt. Dew- in a glass bottle, I will add- and probably buying cigarettes. We were just having a normal conversation, or at least I thought it was normal. I must've been saying the F-word quite a bit because a stranger turned to me, and these words literally changed my life. He said, "I have never heard a young lady speak so terribly in my entire life and use the F-word so frequently in one sentence." The entire store went silent; I could feel my face getting red from embarrassment, and I was moments from passing out and falling down. Regardless of what my mouth sounded like, I was a pretty naïve shy girl, so pointing me out and putting me in some kind of spotlight was devastating. You know in a movie when something dramatic happens and the scenery behind that person goes dark and there's a spotlight on that person? Yeah, that's what I felt like. Now, the theatrics didn't really happen.

50

The store didn't go silent, and the scene didn't fade to black, but it felt like it did. That's all he said, and then he turned around and walked away. To be completely honest, I had no idea that I had even said the F-word once, let alone a few times while I was talking. There were other customers in the gas station and of course, I was embarrassed, but as I started to think about it, I didn't want to be portrayed like that either, and I knew that something needed to change.

Sometimes all it takes is one person to point out something that you're doing, saying, or acting like that will change your life. So many times, we're afraid to speak up and so we just let things slide like it's not our responsibility or problem. I don't know if that man knew Jesus or if he was just mortified by my tongue, but him saying that changed me. Shortly after this, I got saved and started to learn about how powerful our tongues really are. Now the story is about me using swear words, but our words and our tongues can also tear people down by gossiping, slandering, making fun of people, lying, and the list goes on. Matthew 15:10-11 says this: "Jesus called the crowd to him and said listen and understand. What goes into someone's mouth does not defile them, but what comes out of their mouth, that is what defiles them."
Matthew 12:36-37 - "But I tell you that everyone will have to give account on the day of judgment for every empty word that they have spoken. For by your words you'll be acquitted, and by your words you will be condemned."

There is power in the words that we use, we can use them for life or for death. We use them for good or for bad. Words can build a palace or a prison. Our words impact the future. Our words impact others.

Proverbs 16:24 "Kind words are like honey—sweet to the soul and healthy for the body."

Read and Journal.
Day 1: Proverbs 18:21
Day 2: Ephesians 4:29
Day 3: Proverbs 11:9
Day 4: Col 4:6

Day 5: Proverbs 11:12
Day 6: Proverbs 11:17
Day 7: Proverbs 15:1

Write down one thing each day that you are thankful for.

Week 18: Riding in Cars With Strangers

Why did I do the things that I did? I don't know, I'll never have an answer. And really, I don't want to revisit and try to figure it all out. I am just so thankful that God was there the whole time. We make poor choices when we're mad, and we make poor choices when God is not the center of our thoughts. Most of the testimonies in this book are from before I rededicated my life to the Lord when I was 18. However, I knew better. So why is this titled "Riding in Cars With Strangers"? Because that's what I did. I was mad at my boyfriend at the time and so I thought I would get back at him by leaving, throwing a fit, and taking a walk. I don't even remember why we were fighting, and really it doesn't matter. I remember walking down the road about a half mile to a small store, going in, and buying something. At this point, I had calmed down a bit and started to walk back. This man pulled up and asked if I needed a ride. I should've said no. Obviously. What I actually did was say yes and get into his car. What was I thinking?? If my daughters ever did this, I would kill them! (Not really, but you get the point). If my grandchildren did this I would say, "Don't you know right from wrong?! You know better!!" I KNEW BETTER, but I did it anyway.

Since I'm writing this, you know that I'm OK. And the story could've ended up much worse, but it didn't. As we were driving back into town, he put his hand on my leg and asked me if I wanted to go "party." What was this dude thinking? I wasn't for sale! Fight or flight kicked in and I knew I needed to get out of that vehicle as soon as possible. *What have I done? How did I get myself into this?* I told him, "I need you to pull over and let me out right now!" and by the grace of God, he did. He didn't hesitate and stopped the vehicle immediately. I think about the outcome, and I am so shocked that he stopped. I've seen my share of crime documentaries and watched too many news stories that have ended up with the female not surviving or being raped. Nothing happened to me- not a thing. God's hand was on me for sure, there is no doubt of that. I don't think I ever told anyone that I did this until after I was married and I told my husband.

As I was writing this testimony to God's greatness, I thought, "What scriptures will I use to show God's goodness? Knowing right from wrong? God's grace? God's protection? Common sense your parents teach you when you're five?" I was so mad that I made such a poor choice. I acted out of emotions instead of facts. The Lord has given me a sound mind and I needed to start using it. We make poor choices when we let our emotions rule us. We must always be emotionally stable, when upset, sad, mad, or even overjoyed and elated. What does the Bible say about our emotions? "For God gave us a spirit not of fear but of power and love and self-control." - 2 Timothy 1:7

Read and Journal.
Day1: Proverbs 15:18
Day 2: Romans 12:2
Day 3: Ecclesiastes 3:4
Day 4: Romans 12:15
Day 5: 2 Corinthians 10:5
Day 6: Proverbs 29:11
Day 7: Proverbs 25:28

Write down one thing each day that you are thankful for.

Week 19: Vodka is Not Holy Water

This here's a story about my friend "Mike" (not his real name) who, when we were younger, claimed to be a Hare Krishna. I actually had never looked into what this was until I went to write this. When I was younger, I never gave it a thought because it didn't matter to me. I recently have looked into it and understand it to have to do with Hinduism. I never met Mike's parents. I met him through a friend when I was 17. He was odd, peculiar, seemingly unique and he would do and say things that were out of the ordinary to me, but I always thought he was just trying to be different on purpose. I remember asking him if his parents were Hare Krishna as well and he told me no, it was just him, a choice he had made on his own. I remember asking him once if he would go to airports and hand out flowers. That's all I really knew or thought I knew about his newfound religion. He would tell me that we couldn't hurt trees because trees had feelings. He had pages of the Bible taped all over his bedroom walls. He told me once that vodka was holy water so it was okay to drink it and drink lots of it. He would drink, smoke, and cuss, and he was okay with watching any type of movie. I remember going to the movies once with just him and we saw the movie *The Doors*. It was rated R, and I was super uncomfortable most of the movie. It's not that I didn't watch rated R movies at that time, but I didn't watch rated R movies with mixed company because the sex scenes were always so uncomfortable and awkward. We would play with the Ouija board together, and he would tell me stories about witches and warlocks that he knew.

I'm not really sure what was sacred to him. To this day I'm not sure how much of it was true; I don't remember taking any of it as truth, I just thought he was making up stories. He took me once to a tree that he said was special and he called it the "witches' tree." He said that's where he would go to meditate and talk to God. I'm not sure what god he was talking to. One time we were walking out to this witches' tree, which, by the way, was located in Grand Blanc, Michigan. As we were walking to the tree, he told me that the wind would start to pick up the closer we got to the tree, and it did. Every time we went to the tree that's exactly what would happen, even if it was a calm, sunny day the wind would pick up the closer we got. I never gave the enemy the recognition that I believed in what was happening, and I don't know to this day if it was in my mind or it was the power of the enemy. All of this was very uncomfortable to me even before I was saved, I knew right from wrong, I knew God was real and I wasn't going to allow a false god to dictate what I thought or felt or believed.

You're probably asking, "Why did you go in the first place?" The answer is simple- he was my friend. His friends were my friends and I liked hanging out with them. I wasn't afraid of what was going on, but I also didn't believe in it. I thought it was silly, like it was a game. I mean, let's be honest, I was drinking, smoking, and cursing just like they were, I just didn't believe in what he was believing in. Looking back, it was definitely a dangerous road I was on. My life could've gone in so many different directions than the direction that it went. I don't ask a lot of the "why" questions to God because at this point in my life, it doesn't really matter. I'm just thankful that I am in the place that I am now. I will share my testimony in the hopes that it will help somebody else if they find themselves going down the same path.

Somewhere along the line, we lost contact with each other. I have no idea what happened to him or where he is now in his life. I have, however, prayed for him here and there when I think of him. I'm thankful that I have the truth and that I know the one true God.

"Beloved, do not believe every spirit, but test the spirits to see whether they are from God, for many false prophets have gone out into the world." - 1 John 4:1

Read and Journal.
Day 1: Isaiah 43:10
Day 2: Isaiah 45:5
Day 3: Exodus 20:3
Day 4: Exodus 23:13
Day 5: Acts 4:12
Day 6: John 14:6
Day 7: Matthew 24:24

Write down one thing each day that you are thankful for.

Week 20: Holy Spirit Hug

I literally felt the loving arms of Holy Spirit. I was 18, and I believe it was the summer of 1991. You may wonder how or why I can't remember the exact year or moment in time, but back then, we didn't have handy phones to take notes on, and I didn't journal at the time. You'd think we were cavemen. It's nostalgic to think about. Anyways, back to the cool stuff. I had a boyfriend, and I thought he was so amazing. He was everything I ever wanted. He made me feel wanted, pretty, and loved. He and his brother went on a trip to visit their oldest brother's place in a different state. His mom was going to go visit the following week, so she invited me along. Really dramatic long story short, when I got there, he wasn't there. Everyone acted like they didn't know where he had gone off to. Everyone knew, except his mother and I. Truth be told, he had been staying at the neighbor's house with another girl. A lady. A *married* lady at that! The woman's husband knew. I don't know what he was thinking, but somehow husband broke their large front window. I vividly remember the guys singing the song by Annie Lennox *Walking on Broken Glass* like it was some kind of joke.

I was heartbroken. All those moments of feeling wanted, pretty, and loved were gone. Was it all a lie? I felt like it was. I had been heartbroken before, but this time I was devastated and totally embarrassed. Everyone knew what was going on, and I was so humiliated. I think more than anything I was so very embarrassed that someone would think so little of me to treat me that way. I wanted to disappear and not be there any longer. Honestly, I don't remember how long I had to stay there until I got to go home. This wasn't the first time he cheated on me. I was naive and kept trusting him and going back to him.

Looking back on it now, I am totally okay with how it all went down because I am happily married, we have two beautiful daughters, and we get to pour into young adults and build up warriors for Jesus. We are even friends with this guy and his wife today. Weird right? Hindsight is 20/20. Anyway, back to the story.. Before I went home, there was a night I was trying to sleep. I was on the couch where we were staying. I was crying and someone hugged me. I thought it was his cousin giving me a hug because he knew how heartbroken I was. I opened my eyes and no one was there. I still felt arms wrapped tightly around me, holding me. I knew instantly it was the Holy Spirit and He was hugging me and holding me tightly. The longer He held me, the more peace I started to feel until I was no longer crying. I was held like that until I went to sleep. I literally felt Him hold me and He did it because He cared that I was sad. I don't know why He did it except that He cares about what we, care about. He knew that my life would end up good, He knew I would heal and get over it, He knew that we would be civil to each other again one day, He knew I wasn't going to hold anger, hurt, unforgiveness, or bitterness against this person, He knew, but He cared enough to show me in a physical form. I am so thankful for that, and no one can take that from me.

I know that I know that I know God is real! He has shown himself to me too many times for me to deny his love or power. So now it's my turn to show his love and power to you, the reader. He loves you more than you can or will ever comprehend. His love is far deeper and wider than you could ever dream. I think I shared this story just as a testimony of God's goodness and love. I don't know your struggle, hurt, or pain, but I know if you trust and allow God to work within you, all that will subside.

1. What are you thinking about all this?
2. Have you ever experienced anything like this before?
3. Has there been a hard time in your life when you knew God was there with you?
4. How do you deal with hard moments and situations?
5. What steps do you take to go deeper in your walk and relationships with God?

Read and Journal.
Day 1: Spirit of Truth - John 14:17; 15:26; 16:13; 1 John 4:6
Day 2: Spirit of Wisdom - Ephesians 1:17
Day 3: Spirit of Holiness - Romans 1:4
Day 4: Spirit of Faith - 2 Cor 4:13
Day 5: Spirit of Love & Sound Mind - 2 Timothy 1:7
Day 6: Spirit of Grace - Hebrews 10:29
Day 7: Spirit of Adoption - Romans 8:15

Write down one thing each day that you are thankful for.

Week 21: Anger–Cain & Abel

Have you ever been so angry that you wanted to punch something or someone? So mad that you either break down crying or things go flying? So mad the dog runs away from you? What I have learned about myself is that when I get angry, my mouth wants to say very hurtful things. The most hurtful things I could think of to say still were not as bad as I wanted them to be. Why is this? Because hurting people hurt people. Let me say that again… hurting people hurt people. I have learned to control my mouth when I feel angry. You cannot un-ring a bell. You cannot take back words or actions once they happen. Early in our marriage, I was so mad at my husband. Let me tell you, as I write this, I cannot remember why we were even fighting or why I was even mad. All I remember is what I did. I was so angry at him and I'm sure I said things I shouldn't have said. I remember standing in my kitchen and I picked up the first thing I could and I threw it at him. It was a butter knife. He was quick and dodged it; I am very thankful for his cat-like reflexes. It was in that moment that I knew I never wanted to react like that again. I was out of control for sure. If I reside in God then I will have self-control, and that's all I want. We've been married for over 30 years now. I'm happy to say I have never since let anger get the best of me. Have I gotten mad? Oh, heck yes! But now I use words to explain why and how I'm feeling instead of letting the enemy get the best of me.

Cain and Abel's story didn't turn out as good. They both worked in the field. Abel kept flocks and Cain worked the soil. They both brought offerings to the Lord. Cain brought fruits of the soil and Abel brought fat portions from some of the firstborns from this flock. God found favor with Abel's offering but not with Cain's. Cain was angry. The Lord said if you do what is right, it will be acceptable, but if you do not do what is right, sin will be crouching at your door, and it desires to have you and you must rule over it. Instead of taking that to heart, Cain was still angry and did not heed the warning. Cain and Abel went out to the field and Cain attacked and killed his brother Abel. The Lord was asking where his brother was and Cain said, "Am I my brother's keeper?" Then the Lord asked him what he had done and told him that Abel's blood cried out from the ground to him.

Oh my goodness, can you imagine that? He was caught red-handed, literally. And now Cain is under a curse and will work the fields but will not yield what grows from it, and he will wander restlessly on the earth. That does not sound like any way to live. He murdered his brother because he got angry and now his punishment is a curse and to be wandering aimlessly forever. Forever! Genesis 4-read it. Anger is mentioned more than 500 times in scripture. The only emotion mentioned more times than anger is love. Anger first appears in Genesis 4:5 and last appears in Revelation 19:15. Anger is a God-given emotion. What we do in anger determines whether we sin.

 Ever been angry? Of course, you have; we all have. "In your anger do not sin, do not let the sun go down while you are still angry, and do not give the devil a foothold." Ephesians 4:26 The beginning of Ephesians 4 talks about being completely humble and gentle. Be patient, bearing with one another in love. Stay in unity. It talks about speaking the truth in love and it goes on to say we must put off falsehood or lies and speak truthfully. We get angry because we allow another person's actions to bother us. Anger is a normal emotion to have if something is unjust; however, the Bible is clear when it says do not sin in your anger. Cain allowed himself to be so jealous of Abel that he sinned in his anger by murdering his brother. Murdering his brother! Cain's issues were really on him. He should've given God his best, but he did not. Abel did, and God was pleased with Abel. This is when Cain's anger really set in. There are so many things he could've done to control his anger.

Read and Journal.
1. What is your takeaway from what you read today?

2. What things make you angry? Think, meditate on it, and make a list/journal
3. What steps can you take to control your anger so you do not sin?
4. When was the last time you were angry, and how did you handle it? Did you sin in your anger?
5. Is there anyone you need to ask forgiveness from because of your anger? Write that person or people a note asking for their forgiveness, or even better, call them or talk to them in person.

Day 1: Genesis 4:1-7
Day 2: Genesis 4:8-13
Day 3: Genesis 4:14-16
Day 4: Genesis 4:17-20
Day 5: Genesis 4:21-24
Day 6: Genesis 4:25-26
Day 7: Journal and reflect on the last six days and what God has shown you about yourself when dealing with anger.

Lord, we all get angry. Anger is powerful and sometimes scary to us and those with whom we may be angry. Help me to control my anger and follow Your word. I want to have fruitful relationships that are surrounded by love and not the hurt of anger. I will continue to ask for Your insight. Thank You, God, for helping me keep control over my anger. Amen

Write down one thing each day that you are thankful for.

Week 22: Grace

Here's a story of grace. It's just a small, light-hearted story compared to most that are in the Bible, but it was a big story for me because I was newly married. I had never made a full, real meal for someone before, and I had never even done my own laundry. So, the this was very first meal that I made for my husband, who, by the way, is one of seven (and I specify that because they needed lots of food to feed all those kids). Anyway, I served my husband macaroni and cheese. And no, I didn't have anything else to go with it, it was just macaroni and cheese for the main and only dish. There was no steak, no potatoes, no side salad. Just mac & cheese. I for some reason had no clue that macaroni and cheese was not an entire meal. My husband comes home from a long day of painting, takes a shower, and sits down at the dinner table. I was so happy and proud of myself that I made him dinner. He sat down and looked at what was there to eat then looked at me and then looked back at his plate and ever so gently said, "Babe, where is the meat and potatoes? Is there anything else to go with this? You know that macaroni and cheese is a side dish right?" I said with an excited proud tone to my voice, "No, this is what I made you. Doesn't it look good?" Now, in this moment he could've gotten mad and said terrible things about my lack of cooking skills or ability to plan a meal fit for a man, but he didn't. He extended grace to me. He ate his meal ever so happily, but he did let me know that from now on he would like some substance to his meal, some meat every time would be nice, all with a gracious smile. I was very upset. I felt so stupid, not because of what he said. He handled it so gently with me, but I wanted to be the best that I could be and I had to extend grace to myself because I was learning. Then there was the time I was doing laundry. I hadn't really done laundry before. Do you know what happens when you wash white clothes with something red?

That's right, they turn pink. He had pink shirts, he had pink socks, and now pink underwear! Jason, if you read this, thank you so much for not getting mad.

There are so many times in my life that God has had grace on me. Numerous times, my parents have had grace on me, and my friends and my children have given me grace more times than I can remember. I'm given grace by the people I work with when I mess up or do something wrong or forget something. Just as we are given grace, we need to give grace to others when things happen. God has given me grace more times than I can count. Always with me, always giving me grace. Grace is not something we deserve, but God gives it to us anyway. God had grace on Esther when he made her queen. God had grace on Paul when he was given a thorn in his flesh. God spoke to him and said, "My grace is enough," and he was perfect in weakness. In Romans 3, it talks about how no one is righteous. But all are justified by His grace through redemption by Jesus. John came as a witness to testify of God, he was sent by God. Paul experienced God's grace in Romans, Stephen was full of God's grace and faced many trials and challenges. In Ephesians, we are called to unity and maturity. It gives us instructions for living as a Christian. Each of us giving grace as Jesus wanted. And then there is me. God has given me grace many times throughout my life. Grace to forgive, Grace to understand things that are difficult to accept. Grace of God's love. I read a blog about walking in grace. The writer says, "Walking in grace is not just a tagline but it's an invitation." That's not a tagline but an invitation from the Father to share who He is with others. We are saved by grace. Why withhold that from anyone?

"For it is by grace you have been saved, through faith and this is not from yourselves, it is the gift of God. Not by works, so that no one can boast." Ephesians 2:8-9

Read and Journal
Day 1: Esther 2:16-17
Day 2: 2 Corinthians 12:8-9
Day 3: Romans 3:20-24

Day 4: John 1:1-14
Day 5: Romans 1:1-5
Day 6: Acts 6
Day 7: Ephesians 4

Write down one thing each day that you are thankful for.

Week 23: Grade School Friends and Lifelong Connections

This entire testimony is about my sister-in-law, Nichole, and one of my best friends, Marie. Have you ever had those friendships when you were younger that you hoped would last forever, and then you got out of high school and realized that most of them fizzled away? These two girls are the only ones who are still in my life, and for that I am thankful. They know my deepest concerns, the struggles that I've had, and the heartache, but they also know the hope and the victories that I've had, as well. I could tell so many stories about these two, and I'm not sure which ones I should tell and which ones I shouldn't. We've all been through so much together and I've been there through each one of their ups and downs and trials and tribulations. Nichole and I were very good friends before I dated and married her brother. Nikki is the kindest, most genuine person I know. She has always been a loyal friend. She has also been my sister-in-law since 1994. Marie and I met on the school bus when she was in 6th grade and I was in 7th grade. Marie is sensitive, kind, and loves deeply. All three of us have had so many highs and lows as life throws different things at us.

There was a time in our lives when we all kind of stopped hanging out for a season. Nikki moved away to Colorado for a few years before she and her family moved back. We were all choosing and doing different things in our lives. When we were teenagers, we hung out in our little towns of Linden and Fenton. In the 90s, there was a club for underage kids to hang out, dance and play pool. We were there every weekend. We all got married very young, and unfortunately, their marriages didn't last. There were children involved in both of their marriages. The story doesn't stop here; God takes all things and works them out for the good of those who love him. Scripture says, "And we know that in all things God works for the good of those who love him, who have been called according to his purpose." -Romans 8:28. Nikki is now married to an amazing man who adores her and her children. She and her husband also had three kids together. One went to heaven after he was born, and one went to heaven in his early 20s. They know what it's like to trust and depend on God. They have a Godly marriage and love Him with all their hearts. As I write this, Marie is living for God and dating an amazing man. Maybe by the time you read this, they are married. There are a lot of details I left out because it's not my story to tell, it's theirs. Marie wrote a book about her journey through addiction and where she is now with God. You should read it. I want to highlight that God cares for us, in the good and the bad. God has always been right by my side in my friendships. He has been very clear with what friends to keep close and what eyes to let go of. What do lifelong friendships look like? What do Godly friendships look like?

"The one who blesses others is abundantly blessed; those who help others are helped." -Proverbs 11:25 MSG

Read and Journal
Day 1: Luke 6:31
Day 2: Romans 12:10-11
Day 3: Colossians 3:12
Day 4: Hebrews 10:24-25
Day 5: 1 Thessalonians 5:11
Day 6: Psalms 56:8
Day 7: John 15:13

Write down one thing each day that you are thankful for.

Week 24: Party Store Fat Jokes

The year was 1993 when I found out that I was pregnant with my firstborn. My husband and I got married in January 1994, and I was four months pregnant. I know, it's a shock. How could someone who believes in God get pregnant? It really wasn't that difficult. It's easy to find yourself in a predicament that you shouldn't be in in the first place. Around this time, I found out that my sister-in-law was also pregnant. We were both tall and thin. I was 5"7 and at my heaviest 120 pounds; she was just about the same. No one really told me about pregnancy and I didn't think about what was going to happen to my body now that I was growing a human inside of me. I think I gained about 60 pounds with this pregnancy. That was crazy!! About two weeks after I delivered Amber my weight went down to 150. I wasn't thrilled with it because I was 120 for most of my teenage years. I guess I just thought my body was going to go back to what it was. That was a big fat lie for me. So fast forward about 4 1/2 months. Jason and I were visiting his mom where his sister was still living, and she and I went across the street to the party store to get some snacks. We frequently went to this party store, so they knew us very well. They knew that we were both pregnant at the same time and were due around the same time, within four months of each other. By this time my sister-in-law had recently had her baby. So we walked in and we said hello, and they were saying how nice it was to see us and realize we had both had our babies. It was a nice conversation up until this very moment, when one of the guys said to me (referring to my sister-in-law), "She looks great! What happened to you?" My sister-in-law within a week of giving birth was already back down to her original weight. I still was not. I don't remember even responding, I think I just walked out of the store and started crying. I get it, I was thin before I was pregnant, and I am not thin anymore, but to say that to somebody and especially to their face like it's a compliment or an actual question? What the heck?? Who does that?? I have no idea what my sister-in-law said to them after I left, but I remember going back over to the house and my husband asking me what was wrong, and I told him what had happened. He stood up and walked out of the door and walked across the street to the convenience store. I was not sure what was going to happen. Within a few minutes, he came back and said to me, "Come with me, they want to talk to you." I did not want to go back over there! I was mortified and embarrassed. I didn't know if he had a conversation with them in front of all the customers and if there was going to be a crowd there to watch what was going to happen. He made me go. We went back to the store. I don't remember if there was anybody in there, but they apologized and said they never meant to hurt me. I accepted their apology and I left.

I have to this day never been back in that convenience store. It's been 28 years. I should probably make it a point to go in. I asked him what he said, and he told them that they were never to talk to his wife that way and that they owed me an apology. I'm sure there were a few other things that he said, but I'm not really sure what they were. I'm not suggesting that he was cursing at them because he wouldn't do that, but he would give them a lesson on how to treat people. I knew from that day on, that not only did I have a Father in Heaven who defends me, but I had a husband on Earth who would also defend me. If I had even thought that he was going to go across the street to talk to them after I told him what happened, I'm not sure I would've told him. I'm glad, however, that I didn't know and I'm glad that it worked the way that it worked because God taught me a lesson in this. It doesn't matter what other people do or say. We need to remember that people are people regardless of whether they intend to be mean or not. I'm choosing to believe that they didn't mean to be rude.

To counteract a person's words, you need to know who you are in Christ. This particular story shows that I have a defender on earth who loves me like a husband is supposed to. It also shows that I need to know who I am and be secure in who I am. Husbands are to love their wives like God loves the church. I think that God defend His church the same way that my husband defended me. As the church, we need to know who we are in order to reach the lost. We need to be in unity with each other in order for the lost to see that God is good. Our words will either build a palace or a prison depending on what words we use. Honestly, in the moment when this was happening, it felt a lot worse than the reality of it. I didn't look bad, I still looked great for just having a baby. Just didn't know that. I didn't receive that or accept that in my own mind. If you listen to the world too often and too much then your perspective is the world's perspective and not God's.

Do you know who you are? Who is your defender? When you find yourself in situations, who do you go to? After all these years, I feel like if I had known who I was in Christ and I loved myself enough, I'm not sure I would have run back to my husband the way that I did. At this point in my life, I was still comparing myself to Jason's perfectly shaped and beautiful sisters. There are four of them, they all have more than two children and are tall and thin to this day. You cannot compare yourself to other people. It will either make you feel better or worse depending on what you're comparing. That is not what God called us to do. You are a beautiful you. I can honestly say at this point in my life, at 48 years old at the time I'm writing this, that I love me. I am not the weight that I want to be, but I love who I am and I love what I look like. The only thing that matters is if I am loving people the way that God called me to love people, that I am defending people the way that God has called me to defend people.

One of the things that I started doing after I realized how important wisdom is was to start praying for wisdom. So I suggest that you start praying for wisdom every day. Wisdom teaches you when to confront something, wisdom teaches you when to let it go, wisdom teaches you right from wrong, wisdom is smarter than our feelings. Wisdom is so important. If I had been walking in wisdom when this happened, I could've dealt with it within myself and let it go like I do now with situations. I don't know if God wanted my husband to go over there and do what he did, but I do know that God used it. God, through Jason, taught them a lesson in how to treat people, which I believe was wisdom. We are going to go through some verses about wisdom and defending this week. Proverbs 21:3 says, "To do righteousness and justice is more acceptable to the Lord than sacrifice." Proverbs 21:15 says, "When justice is done, it is a joy to the righteous but tear to evildoers."

Read and Journal.
Day 1: Proverbs 21:2
Day 2: Proverbs 21:4
Day 3: Proverbs 1:3
Day 4: Acts 20:28
Day 5: John 14:17
Day 6: Proverbs 28:5
Day 7: John 19:30

Write down one thing each day that you are thankful for.

Week 25: Angels Sang Me to Sleep

I know many people are skeptical of the supernatural, or you've seen preachers on TV who look like they pump things up to be something they're not. I get it- some things seem too good to be true. I've watched programs or heard stories and thought, "Yeah right, that didn't happen," or that their perception of this situation is totally off. But then I experienced it for myself. I believe the year was 1995 or '96, somewhere around then. Myself, my friend Marie, and some others went to a Benny Hinn Crusade in Detroit. I've seen him on TV and I've seen the outrageous stuff- people falling down from the Holy Spirit or being healed and standing up and walking from a wheelchair- so I knew what I was in for. I wanted to believe it was real, but how? How can that be true?

So I went with the thought that I was going to find out how true this all was. I was doubtful and wasn't going to act like something was happening if it wasn't. So Marie and I were standing during worship, singing and enjoying our time. I started smelling something that was so pretty, something sweet and inviting. I remember my mother-in-law telling me that the Lord has a fragrance. "Follow God's example, therefore, as dearly loved children and walk in the way of love, just as Christ loved us and gave himself up for us as a fragrant offering and sacrifice to God." -Ephesians 5:1-2 NIV. There are several scriptures that talk about the fragrance of God. So I looked at my friend Marie, then I looked around to see if someone was putting on perfume and everyone was worshiping, arms raised and eyes closed. I tapped her on the shoulder and said, "Hey, do you smell that"? Marie looked at me confused, smiled, and said, "Smell what?" I said, "That sweet smell, kinda like roses?" She said, "No, I don't smell anything." So I looked at the lady next to me and asked her. Let's remember I don't know the lady next to me. She looked at me, smiled, and said, "No, I don't smell anything, but if you do, that's God's sweet aroma, so bask in it for as long as you can." So I did just that. I stood there with my eyes shut and just soaked it all in. I could smell Him, and I never wanted it to go away. It eventually faded, but don't worry, this story gets better.

Service happens and at the end of the evening, the praying and healing portion starts. This was it- was this all real or what? I was about to find out. If you have never seen Benny Hinn, YouTube him so you know what I was in the middle of. So he was praying for people and it appeared that they were being healed. Blind eyes opening, the crippled standing and walking, miracle after miracle. *How am I to know if it's real, God? I want to know!* So it came to a time when Benny was praying over the entire stadium and said, "God wants you to experience the Holy Spirit, so everyone stand in this place. No more doubting. I'm going to pray, and Holy Spirit is going to go out and start on the right side and go all the way around to the left side and He is going to touch you." I looked at my friend and said, "Don't fall down just because everyone around us will. This has to be real or we won't do it." She agreed. Starting on the right side of the stadium, people started falling back into their seats from being hit by the power of the Spirit. I wasn't just going to fall for show. I didn't care if I was the only one left standing. This was going to be God or I'm not doing it. What do you think happened? Did my doubt leave me standing there by myself or did I sit down because I didn't want to be embarrassed? Well, it was real. Holy Spirit hit me and He set me down back into my seat. Not violently, but I felt the power.

We haven't gotten to the most amazing part yet. So I was in amazement of the thing that I'd just experienced, and as we were walking out of the stadium back to our cars everyone was singing, "Alleluia." Just that, over and over and over again. It was beautiful. I got home that night and Jason was still awake. I told him everything I experienced. As I lay down to go to sleep, I shut my eyes and I heard in my ears, "Alleluia, Alleluia, Alleluia, Alleluia." I opened my eyes and looked at Jason. His eyes were shut. I said, "Hey, babe...do you hear that?" He said, "Hear what?" I said, "I can hear angels singing in my ears; they are singing 'Alleluia' over and over again." He said, "Just enjoy it," smiled, and shut his eyes again. So I did. I lay there and enjoyed it. They sang me to sleep. It was an amazing experience, a testimony no one can take away from me.

It's real, God is real, and His power is real. Believe that it's real and walk in it.

"But God made the earth by his power, and he preserves it by his wisdom. With his own understanding, he stretched out the heavens. When he speaks in the thunder, the heavens roar with rain. He causes the clouds to rise over the earth. He sends the lightning with the rain and releases the wind from his storehouses." Jeremiah 10:12-13

If my research is correct, there are 83 documented miracles in the Old Testament and 81 documented miracles in the New Testament.

1. Do you believe in the supernatural miracles that happen today? If so why?
2. If not, is it something you struggle to believe is real?
3. Are signs and wonders something you desire to see in your relationship with God?
4. Have you ever experienced the supernatural? If so, write down what you experienced.
5. Do you know someone who needs to experience the supernatural? If so, pray that God will reveal His wonders to them. 1 Corinthians 12:31 says, "Now eagerly desire the greater gifts."

Read and Journal.
Day 1: Psalm 147:4-5
Day 2: Jeremiah 10:12-13
Day 3: Luke 5:15
Day 4: Romans 1:20
Day 5: Luke 1:35
Day 6: Hebrews 1:3
Day 7: Colossians 2:12
Write down one thing each day that you are thankful for.

Week 26: Trust

Trust - noun 1. Reliance on the integrity, strength, ability, surety, etc. of a person or thing; confidence 2. A person on whom or thing on which one realizes.

God is my trust! God is my trust! Written in black-and-white in Webster's dictionary for the world to see. My trust was put to the test in one of the hardest times of my life (yes I said one, this girl has many testimonies of God's grace and I'd love to share, but for today I'll tell you about God being my trust.) I was 24; it was the end of November 1997. I was about 10 weeks pregnant with Kelli Jordan McKay. I started having some cramps. Shortly after the cramping came, there was blood- bright red blood. My heart sank. This was not supposed to be happening. There was a significant amount of cramping and blood. I called my midwife right away. She called my doctor, and from what I explained to them about what was happening with my body, they told me I was having a miscarriage. A miscarriage? Me? I don't think so. Not me. The tears began to flow. It was a Friday. They told me to rest for the weekend and on Monday they would do a D&C and clean out my body. I called my husband home from work and after talking with him, our parents, and our pastors, we decided before I got a D&C, we needed an ultrasound to make sure. I believe in prayer, I believe in miracles, and I trust God. We prayed for God's will to be done and all glory to Him. No matter what the outcome would be, I chose to trust Him. I had complete peace come over me in the situation. I still had cramps and blood show all weekend, but I continued to trust God no matter what.

Monday morning came and my husband went to the midwife's office with me. The doctor was very nice and compassionate but assured us that unfortunately he sees this all the time and was preparing us for the worst. As he started the ultrasound he said, "Huh. Hmm. Ha, wow, well, Merry Christmas, because this baby has a very strong heartbeat." I looked over at the screen and looking back at us were these little eyes that blinked twice as if to say, "Hello, mommy." We praised God and told the doctor we had been praying all weekend for life. This was a miracle, but it wasn't the end of the story.

Throughout my entire pregnancy with Kelli, my blood work never showed that I was more than 10 weeks along. She died, and God brought her back to life. Let that sink in. She died and God breathed life back into her. My nurse referred to me as "the girl with the weird blood," and I got to share what happened time and time again. Kelli Jordan is a miracle, and God brought her to life twice because the enemy doesn't get to win. I continued to have cramps and blood show here and there throughout my entire pregnancy. Today, she is in her 20s, married with her own baby, and working with us in ministry. I know not every story turns out like this, and I am so sorry. I don't know why, and I wish I could tell you why. I do know God is a good God and He loves you and your babies. God gives life, He doesn't take it away. My story is a story about trust. I was trusting Him in the storm no matter what. My heart and mind were prepared for the worst, but I was still trusting in God that He knew what was best.

"But Jesus immediately said to them: 'Take courage! It is I. Don't be afraid.' 'Lord, if it's you,' Peter replied, 'tell me to come to you on the water.' 'Come,' he said. Then Peter got down out of the boat, walked on the water, and came toward Jesus. But when he saw the wind, he was afraid and, beginning to sink, cried out, 'Lord, save me!' Immediately Jesus reached out his hand and caught him. 'You of little faith' he said, 'Why did you doubt?'" Matthew 14:27-31

I can 100% say that I did not sink on the water, not because God brought my baby back to life, but because I was trusting Him 100%. I know that at any time, my children or my loved ones can be taken from me. I am prepared for those things to happen. That doesn't mean that I won't be sad, but I trust God and I don't blame God for the bad things that happen in this world. We live on Earth, and this is the world. This is by no means heaven.

Day 1: Journal about a time you trusted or needed to trust God.
Day 2: Mark 4:34-41 - caught in a storm in the middle of the sea of Galilee. Fear and doubt slip in. Jesus was asleep. Journal about a time you had trust and faith in what you did to achieve it.
Day 3: John 16:33 -in the world, you will have tribulation, but Jesus has come to overcome the world. Journal how you have allowed Jesus to overcome things in your life.
Day 4: Peace! Be still! Read Mark 4:39 and journal about a time Jesus displayed this over your life.
Day 5: Mark 4:40 Jesus rebuked the wind and the waves but also the disciples for their unbelief. Journal about a time Jesus did this for you and what you learned from it.
Day 6: Read Isaiah 41:10 and journal about God's love, care, and concern for you even when it feels like everything around you is falling apart.
Day 7: Today, I want you to journal and reflect back on the week and thank God for other things and times He has been with you in the midst of the storm.

Write down one thing each day that you are thankful for.

Week 27: Fasting

What is fasting, why do we do it, and how? Fasting is the willing abstinence or reduction from some or all food, drink, or both, for a period of time. I remember the first time I tried fasting, I believe I lasted five hours. The longest five hours of my life at that point. Ever notice that when you want to do something to honor God it becomes almost impossible? There have been many times before when I would skip breakfast and lunch because I either forgot to eat- yeah, it happens to me- or I was busy and I lost track of time. I wasn't fasting on purpose, but I was denying myself food because I was busy. Then you realize, wow, I'm hungry, and you finally eat. When you fast for a purpose, you are well aware, and the enemy comes at you like a roaring lion wanting to destroy you just like the Bible states. I sleep longer than five hours a night and I'm not eating while I sleep, but that first time I fasted was hard. It was hard because the enemy knew I had a purpose, and through prayer and fasting I was going to make a difference and he was scared. The second time I fasted, I was mentally prepared and determined. God called me to fast for a week. During the time when I would normally be eating breakfast, lunch, or dinner I would be praying and speaking truth over the situation for which I was fasting. The first few days were very hard while fighting my flesh and tummy growls. I remember quoting scripture and saying, "No, you will not win. I will beat my flesh and make it my slave. I am not a slave to my flesh, I will pray and fast and my family will be set free," and I would repeat that every time that feeling or thought would arise. It helped a lot. After I got past the first three days it became easy to lay down and I was able to focus more on the prize and the reason why I was doing it. I can't tell you if my fasting helped my family members or changed their lives at all. I do know that I was obedient in what I was called to do, and I might never know this side of heaven, but I firmly believe that prayer and fasting changes things. Only God really knows, and that's fine with me. "No, I strike a blow to my body and make it my slave so that after I have preached to others, I myself will not be disqualified for the prize." - 1 Corinthians 9:27.

What does the Bible say about fasting? When we fast and pray, it can help us hear from God or reveal hidden sin. Fasting can help as you stand in the gap for someone else. Fasting and prayer can make your relationship with God stronger. Fasting and prayer can be a teacher to us in many ways. It can teach us to pray, strengthen our faith, fill us with joy, and be an example to others. In Matthew 17, fasting and prayer is required to cast out a demon. The Bible talks about different types of fasting- limiting yourself to different types of food, fasting from food and/or water, fasting from sex. It's important to know your motives about why you are fasting. When we fast, there should be a reason. Ultimately, if it is going to bring me closer to God, then I'm going to do it. "When you fast, do not look somber as the hypocrites do, for they disfigure their faces to show men they are fasting. I tell you the truth, they have received their reward in full. But when you fast, put oil on your head and wash your face, so that it will not be obvious to men that you are fasting, but only to your Father, who is unseen; and your Father, who sees what is done in secret, will reward you." - Matthew 6:16-18

1. Have you ever fasted before? If so for how long and for what reason?
2. Do you feel like fasting was beneficial to you? If so how?
3. Do you feel like fasting was beneficial to others? If so how?
4. Is fasting a part of your walk with Jesus?
5. Are you more likely now to pray and fast more?

Read and Journal.
Day 1: Daniel 1:8-14
Day 2: Daniel 10:2-3
Day 3: Luke 4:2
Day 4: Acts 9:9

Day 5: Exodus 19:15
Day 6: 1 Corinthians 7:5
Day 7: Esther 4:16

Write down one thing each day that you are thankful for.

Week 28: Encouragement

When we started serving as leaders at our church in 2000, Dena (who happens to be married to our lead pastor and is the greatest encourager you could ever meet) started writing me these cards that I would get now and then. I didn't think much of it at first until one day it hit me. These cards were changing my life; they were changing me. They were filled with the truth of who God says I am. They were filled with the most encouraging words and it was changing my view of myself and of other people. They meant so much to me, and I have kept every single card she has ever written to me. My heart so wanted to do that for people. I wanted to give other people the gift she was giving to me. So what did I do? I mimicked what Dena was doing. I started writing notes and cards to our leaders and students. I would call out all the amazing things God saw in them. I would speak life. I may never know the impact it made on those who served with me in youth ministry or the students, but I know the impact it made on me when I got those cards from Dena. I still get them from her, and they still encourage my heart and remind me of who God says I am.

This is now one of my favorite things to do for people. I love calling out greatness and purpose in people. I love pushing people toward their calling and helping people to find and understand their giftings. I love reminding people who God says they are. It's easy for me to lift others up; however, as much as I was doing it for others, I wasn't encouraging myself. So, I decided to change that. I am responsible for my walk with Jesus, and if I am encouraged and I walk in that, then doing it for others will be that much more powerful and effective. I had not even considered encouraging myself- it was not a thought in my mind palace (that's what I call my mind.) How did I learn to encourage myself? It's easier than you think. I started speaking life over myself and speaking truth into my own life! This takes me back to why I call my mind a palace. I am a Queen, given a crown by my heavenly Father. With that comes the responsibility to keep my mind pure. It's a palace and I need to keep it well-kept because I am royalty. I didn't always believe that, so I started speaking that truth over myself. I am royalty, I am beautifully designed, I am fearfully and wonderfully made, I have purpose, I am a Queen and I wear a great crown. Speak truth over yourself today and don't stop speaking it.

Take this time to journal all the things God says to you as encouragement. Who does God say you are? What is He calling you to do? Journal the things God is speaking to you.

"Those that seek the Lord lack no good thing." - Psalm 34:10

Think of 5 people you'd like to encourage. Write their names down and write each of them a card full of encouragement.

Read and Journal.
Day 1: 1 Thessalonians 5:11
Day 2: Deuteronomy 31:8
Day 3: Psalm 55:22
Day 4: Psalm 121:1-2
Day 5: Psalm 46:1
Day 6: Psalm 23:4
Day 7: John 16:33

Write down one thing each day that you are thankful for.

Week 29: Giving

"Remember this: whoever sows sparingly will also reap sparingly, and whoever sows generously will also reap generously. Each of you should give what you have decided in your hearts to give, not reluctantly or under compulsions, for God loves a cheerful giver. And God is able to bless you abundantly, so that in all things at all times, having all that you need, you will abound in every good work." - 2 Corinthians 9:6-8

I happen to love giving. I find joy in giving gifts for birthdays, holidays, or just because. I find joy in giving in the offering to support a missionary or a ministry. I want to be in a place to be able to bless people in need. I absolutely love it. However, I haven't always loved it. There was a time that I dreaded it. I would even go so far as to say that I actually hated it. Not only did I not understand giving, I couldn't afford to give. I couldn't afford it in my head or on paper but I couldn't afford in my heart and spiritual walk not to give. Then I heard a teaching about giving and tithing, and with faith and trust as we started doing this, things started to change. We started tithing before we did anything else with our paychecks. We made a budget, we wrote down all money coming in and then wrote down all money going out. We gave tithe and offering before we paid any bill. It wasn't long until things started to fall into place. Our finances changed in a way that only God could've done. Being obedient to God's word is so worth it. Be obedient, even if you are afraid.

When we started tithing and giving before we knew it, we were being blessed in our finances. My dad was the one that taught me how to budget. He is and always has been very good with finances. He did not understand why I would tithe and give before I paid any bill I had. I told him I wanted to honor God and he would take care of the rest.

My dad watched this unfold over a few years before he became a believer in this. Our bills were paid on time and not only that we would get money from unexpected places. I'm not even going to try to explain it because I can't. I can however say that God is good and always takes care of us. We have been blessed by people taking us out for dinner and a Broadway show. People giving us their cabin up north for the weekend just to get away. The list goes on. We don't give to get; we give to be obedient to God.

I don't totally understand all the wonders of God, but tithing and giving bring so much joy. God loves a cheerful giver. Ever heard of the widow's offering in the Bible? There was this woman who wanted to give even though she didn't have a lot to give. The rich gave out of their wealth, but she gave out of her poverty and put in everything she had. We give, not because God needs our money but because those that are in need do. We are called to help the less fortunate, even when we think they don't deserve it.

"Jesus sat down opposite the place where the offerings were put and watched the crowd putting their money into the temple treasury. Many rich people threw in large amounts. But a poor widow came and put in two very small copper coins, worth only a few cents. Calling his disciples to him, Jesus said, "Truly I tell you, this poor widow has put more into the treasury than all the others. They all gave out of their wealth; but she, out of her poverty, put in everything—all she had to live on." Mark 12:41-44 NIV

What does giving look like to you?

Read and Journal.
Day 1: Deuteronomy 15:10
Day 2: Deuteronomy 16:7
Day 3: Proverbs 3:27
Day 4: Proverbs 11:24-25
Day 5: Proverbs 21:26
Day 6: Proverbs 22:9
Day 7: Proverbs 28:27

Write down one thing each day that you are thankful for.

Week 30: Go and Sin No More

"Jesus went to the Mount of Olives. Early in the morning he came again to the temple. All the people came to him, and he sat down and taught them. The scribes and the Pharisees brought a woman who had been caught in adultery, and placing her in the midst they said to him, 'Teacher, this woman has been caught in the act of adultery. Now in the Law, Moses commanded us to stone such women. So what do you say?' This they said to test him, that they might have some charge to bring against him. Jesus bent down and wrote with his finger on the ground. And as they continued to ask him, he stood up and said to them, 'Let him who is without sin among you be the first to throw a stone at her.' And once more he bent down and wrote on the ground. But when they heard it, they went away one by one, beginning with the older ones, and Jesus was left alone with the woman standing before him. Jesus stood up and said to her, 'Woman, where are they? Has no one condemned you?' She said, 'No one, Lord.' And Jesus said, 'Neither do I condemn you; go, and from now on sin no more.' John 8:1-11 ESV

It was early 2000. I was 27 and had two small children. The girls were one and five. I was lonely and felt neglected. My feelings were telling me that my husband of almost 7 years didn't want to spend time with me or the kids. I had felt this way for about a year at this point. He worked two jobs- not because he needed to, but because he wanted to. He would work his night job and then any free time he had he would work with his dad in the family business. I wanted the free time to be spent with us. I wanted him to want to be with me. I was so tired of begging him to pay attention to me. He would play with the girls before dinner but quality time with me was few and far between. I eventually and slowly disconnected. I was numb. I didn't care anymore. I started to feel a lot of resentment, bitterness, anger, and hatred towards him. It got to where I didn't care how long he worked. I would get irritated knowing that he was coming home because I was used to being by myself and him coming home felt like an invasion of my space and routine.

I allowed the enemy to speak into my life so much that I finally went looking for approval and love somewhere else. I convinced myself that if he didn't love me, I would find someone who would, and that's just what I did (or at least that is what I thought I did). In that moment of rebellious disobedience, I broke our marriage covenant. I just wanted to be wanted. In doing this, I was not trusting God with my marriage, and I was not trusting my husband to love me correctly. One day at dinner, I looked at my husband and I said, "I'm not happy. I don't feel like you care, and I think we need to separate." He looked at me and asked, "Have you been seeing someone else?" At this moment, I could have lied and simply said I just wanted out of this marriage or come up with a million other excuses, but I didn't want to lie. I said, "Yes."

This is when a whirlwind of emotions started. I don't even remember it all fully. I just know I was empty, I had no life left, my soul was dark, and my spirit was disconnected. I wanted to die. I told him how I felt distant from him, how it seemed like he never wanted to be around me or spend time with me. I felt like I was always last on his list and everything and everyone else was put before me. I felt like a single married mom who was playing house while he did whatever he wanted, and I was done playing. I knew at this moment he was going to tell me to pack up my stuff and leave and never come back. But that's not how this story ends.

He looked at me and said, "Before you leave, I want you to ask God what you are supposed to do and then do what He says." I knew instantly what God was saying, and I wanted to sit there quietly for hours, but I blurted out, "God wants me to stay! And I will, but I don't want to be here!" I know that me staying is what he wanted to hear, but I know that it hurt him to hear that I didn't want to stay. Through hours of conversation, he told me his side of the situation was not to spend so much time away from us but that he was working all the extra hours to help us financially. He was working hard for us, for it to be better, not worse. He was unaware and blind to my needs and didn't have an understanding that I wanted his time, not his money. On the other hand, I was unaware and blind to his needs, and I didn't have an understanding that he was doing the best he could to not only support his family but to help his dad in the process. I reminded him of something I have always said to him- that I would follow him anywhere God led him, and that if I had to, I would sleep in a cardboard box just to have the quality time with him.

We started going to marriage counseling and went for about a year. There was a lot of give and take during these times and learning who we were in Jesus and who Jesus was to us in our marriage. I can now say that we have a very strong marriage. We have been able to use our hurts to help others going through similar situations. I have lost count of the marriages God has allowed us to minister to. God turns ashes into beauty. What the enemy tried to destroy, God has made stronger.

As I write this, I feel as if I am making up a story of some unknown couple. I don't know this insecure, lost, and lonely girl. That's not who I am anymore. I am redeemed and set free. I am forgiven not only by my gracious husband but by my merciful Father in Heaven. And Jesus said, "Neither do I condemn you; go, and from now on sin no more." Have I walked in shame? Yes, I have. Even to this day, the enemy tries to throw shame at me continually in attempts to stop me from ministering to others. I have to quite often say, "I am not what I have done; I am forgiven and redeemed no matter what any human says." In Romans 10:10 it says, "For it is with your heart that you believe and are justified, and it is with your mouth that you profess your faith and are saved." I need to be continually professing my faith. My pastor recently taught on this, and this is directly from my notes:

*Because of what Jesus has done for you... You are no longer what you've done.

*Because of what Jesus has done for you… You are not what others have done to you.

*Because of what Jesus has done for you… You are not slaves of the opinions, judgments, and preferences of others.

I so needed to hear that. I needed that confirmation to push me to write this devotional. It's raw, real, revealing, and frankly, quite terrifying because many may judge, have opinions, and think they know best, much like I do from time to time. So I pray, "Lord take that judgmental spirit from me so that I don't lay shame on others. Allow me to see them the way you see them and how you see me. AMEN!"

Some more from my notes…

*So who are you? You are His, You are the best thing God has ever done for you.

*You have a divine purpose! You are God's answer, solution, and provision for your generation.

Read and Journal.
Day 1: John 8:1-11
Day 2: Romans 10:9-11
Day 3: 1 John 3:20
Day 4: Galatians 5:13
Day 5: Romans 6:7
Day 6: Romans 13:8
Day 7: 2 Corinthians 3:17

Write down one thing each day that you are thankful for.

Week 31: How to be BOLD

I was introduced to this concept of God, Jesus, and the Holy Spirit when I was young. I thought I understood it- God and all His angels live in heaven, Satan and all his evil little demons live in hell, which is obviously in the middle of the earth. If I was good, I would go to heaven, and if I was bad, I would go to hell. I was good! I'd never killed anyone, I didn't go around robbing banks or stealing other people's cats, even though I am most definitely sure I wanted to take a cat or two home, but I didn't! So clearly, I'm going to heaven! Don't just assume because someone told you something about God that it's the truth. You must search and seek for yourself. Thankfully, I've since learned that that's not how it works. Unfortunately, there are "good" people who don't know Jesus and "bad" ones that do. It's an upside-down, inside-out concept that we as humans have a hard time understanding. I met Jesus when I was young- I believe I was 5. I asked Him to be the King of my heart, but this intimate relationship didn't start with Him until I was much older. I even rededicated my life at 18, but the relationship part didn't start until I was 28. I started this journey of wanting to know Him. I had watched others flourish in their relationship with Jesus and I wanted that. I longed for intimacy with the Father. I didn't know how to do that until I was taught. It's like a baby learning to feed themselves. It was a slow process. How did I do it? I sought it out. I looked for a mentor to teach me. Once you have that then you start applying it to your life. It's really that simple. Read the Bible and then do what it says. Read the Bible and apply it to your life. Let me say it again- read the Bible and then do what it says. Apply it to your life. That's how you make good choices; you take the situation and see if it lines up with the word of God. It honestly comes down to a choice. We have free will and we make a choice. We need to be bold for Him. There was an article I read by

90

Billy Graham; if you don't know who that is, look him up; you won't be disappointed. He had an acronym, and the word was BOLD which stood for Believe, Obey, Learn and Declare. Basically it was this: Believe what God declares. Let the bible speak for itself (Hebrews 4:12). All we have to do is believe it. Obey His commandments. What are God's commandments? Learn them, then live by them. Learn from the Word. The Bible is full of so much about us as humans, the good, the bad, and everything in between. We need to learn from all of it. We lack knowledge, but God is good and faithful to teach us what we need to know (1 Corinthians 10:11). Declare God's promises. We need to read the word to know what these promises are and then live by it. His word is for our good, not His. So many times people assume God wants us to have all these rules so He feels superior. He doesn't need to feel superior. He already is, always has been, and always will be. He has these for us so that we can live in joy and have an abundant life. It's good for us and helps us to live a long life worth living. Read and do what it says.

I recently read this scripture: "Down the road in Joppa there was a disciple named Tabitha. She was well-known for doing good and helping out. During the time Peter was in the area she became sick and died. Her friends prepared her body for burial and put her in a cool room. Some of the disciples had heard that Peter was visiting in Lydda and sent two men to ask if he would be so kind as to come over. Peter got right up and went with them. They took him into the room where Tabitha's body was laid out. Her old friends, most of them widows, were in the room mourning. They showed Peter pieces of clothing that were made while she was with them. Peter put the widows all out of the room. He knelt and prayed. Then he spoke directly to the body: 'Tabitha, get up.' She opened her eyes. When she saw Peter, she sat up. He took her hand and helped her up. Then he called in the believers and widows, and presented her to them alive. When this became known all over Joppa, many put their trust in the Master. Peter stayed for a long time in Joppa as a guest of Simon the Tanner." Acts 9:36-37, 40-43 MSG

We say we are Christians, we say we believe in God, we say we believe what the Bible says, yet we doubt so often. Peter says, "Hey, Tabby, get up," as if she isn't dead. And she does. And she's like, "Oh, hi." WHAT???? She was dead and now she isn't because Peter had power and faith. I WANT THAT FAITH!! Peter knew what to do and did it. He was taught and applied it. Let's stop doubting and start walking it out!! Amen

Read and Journal.
Day 1: Luke 10:25-37
Day 2: James 1:20-25
Day 3: Psalms 119:105
Day 4: James 1:22
Day 5: Isaiah 40:8
Day 6: Psalms 18:30
Day 7: Psalms 119:130

Ask yourself these questions as you study these scriptures: How does this passage apply to my life? What changes must I make? How will I carry out these changes? What will be my personal prayer concerning this truth? Which verse or verses in this section should I memorize? What illustration or word picture will help me remember what I've read?

Write down one thing each day that you are thankful for.

Week 32: The Importance of God's Word

I got saved when I was 18, I wasn't really taught that I should be reading the Word every day. Yes, people said I should read my Bible, but there was no discipleship in it. I would read it here and there but most of my days were filled with things I wanted to do, what I wanted to watch, read, play, or those sorts of behaviors. I didn't daily apply God's word to my life until I got involved in ministry. I wasted so much time that I could've been filling myself with God instead of things of this world. I'm telling you this so that you will from now on be soaked in his presence and his word every single day. Do not let a day go by that you are not reading the Bible or learning more about him. Imagine that you had a mirror and not just any ordinary mirror but a mirror that only told you the truth. Like the magic mirror the wicked Queen had in Snow White only we aren't wicked, we are righteous. Okay, are you with me? This mirror only tells you the truth about who you are, what you look like, what you should say, do and feel in every situation. You might think that the mirror you have at home shows you what you look like, but it really doesn't, not really. Not the way God sees you anyway. Physically or spiritually. He sees us differently than we see ourselves. So you have been given the gift of this amazing mirror, but we don't often take the opportunity to allow it to speak to us, and very seldom do we believe it. That's the key, you need to believe what the mirror is saying to you. It speaks truths about who you are and that needs to find deep, deep roots within your heart. What is this mirror? If you haven't figured it out by now, this mirror is the Word of God. It speaks truths, lots and lots and lots of truths. Stories, parables, lessons, declarations, devotions, and teachings. What a beautiful mirror of how God is showing us to live and walk in truths about ourselves. I am overwhelmed by His love. It is because of His words that I can get through each day. I am so thankful for His Word and what it does for me in my life.

Read all of Psalm 119 and declare it over yourself. Believe and walk in it!!

Read and Journal.
Day 1. Psalm 119:11
Day 2. 2 Peter 3:18
Day 3. 2 Timothy 3:16
Day 4. Hebrews 4:12
Day 5: Psalm 119:105
Day 6: John 17:3
Day 7: Take today and journal about the importance of reading and applying the word every day

Write down one thing each day that you are thankful for.

Week 33: Forgiveness

Forgiveness is mentioned 144 times in the NIV Bible. What does forgiveness look like? How do you forgive someone who has hurt you?

Many years ago when my husband and I were youth pastors, there was a young lady in our youth group who came from a not-so-ideal upbringing. She hadn't seen her mom in many years, and her dad drank often. There were several times that he wouldn't pick her up from youth and we took her home, or he would show up to get her and it was clear that he had been drinking and we would have to call the police. After some things transpired, she was taken out of the home. There was no family available to take her in, so my husband and I did. Our two daughters were 6 and 10 at the time. This young lady was 14. She was in our home and like a daughter to us for 5 years. She moved out at 19. A lot of different things happened along the way while she lived with us. I knew she was hurting because her mom wasn't around and her dad wasn't taking the steps to get her back. She was also diagnosed with borderline personality disorder. We did our very best to raise her and help her heal. To make a long story short, this young lady that we brought into our home and called "daughter" started telling people, family, friends, and church friends lies about us. We are very much who we are in and out of our home. Those who know us know these lies are not true. But there were a few people who believed some of the things she was saying. After many conversations, we also found out that she was telling one of our daughters lies as well. Things like we didn't really love her as much as we loved her younger sister. Stuff like that. I don't want to paint a picture of this young girl being terrible, but the truth is she was hurting, and hurting people hurt people.

After talking to professionals and researching border personality disorder, her actions made more sense to us. We ended up parting ways and creating boundaries. I was angry and hurt- so very hurt. I loved her like my own. It took me many, many years to find forgiveness. I had to realize that my unforgiveness wasn't hurting anyone except me. Finding forgiveness was a journey between God and me. Forgiveness is a choice, not a feeling. I chose to forgive her. There were times I had to choose to forgive her every day. That doesn't mean I allowed her back into our life. I had to have and keep boundaries. It's okay to choose to forgive someone and keep boundaries in place.

Many years after we parted ways, we tried to reconcile, but she wasn't in a place spiritually to do that. We are not in contact with each other, but I can honestly say that I have no hard feelings toward her. I found forgiveness, and we still love her.

"For if you forgive other people when they sin against you, your heavenly father will also forgive you. But if you do not forgive others their sins, your father will not forgive you your sins." Matthew 6:14-15

1. Is there someone (or several someones) in your life that you need to forgive? If so, write them down.
2. Start praying for this person/people and ask for God's grace to forgive. Forgive them every day if you need to.
3. What steps will you take towards forgiveness?
4. What does God's forgiveness for us look like?
5. Pray for a friend or family member who needs to forgive someone. Encourage them with a text or call.

Read and Journal.
Day 1: Read Colossians 3:13.
Day 2: Read Ephesians 4:31-32.
Day 3: Read John 1:9.
Day 4: Read Isaiah 43:25-26.
Day 5: Read Acts 3:19
Day 6: Read Ephesians 1:7
Day 7: Read Hebrews 10:17

Apply forgiveness daily!

Write down one thing each day that you are thankful for.

Week 34: Friendship

What does a godly friendship look like? When I was younger- middle school and high school age- I remember having a few girlfriends, but those friendships weren't healthy. I didn't know that at the time. I wish I did! I've had three best friends. I had a friend during my middle school days, and we were always together, day after day after day. If I wasn't with her, I felt anxious. If she hung out with someone else without me, I would get so jealous. The same thing happened when I was in high school but with a different friend. I know those friendships were unhealthy on my part. They were amazing girls, but I didn't know how to have healthy friendships. Now that I'm older and I know what friendship looks like, I know that those friendships were not healthy. Did we have fun together? Oh yeah, a lot of fun. Those are some of my very best memories, but I didn't know that those were not healthy friendships for me. A healthy friendship doesn't involve jealousy or being anxious because they're with somebody else. That's an obsession and insecurity with myself that I couldn't allow my friend to have other friends. The first red flag is when you get angry, jealous, or anxious if your friend has other friends or friendships. You could have an unhealthy soul tie with somebody if this is the type of friendship you have.

I even at one point in my life had an unhealthy soul tie with my husband. I know that sounds impossible, but God showed me this one year when my husband was on a missions trip to Mexico. I was so sad he was gone and I shut down emotionally. I told no one. The entire week he was gone, I literally just stayed at home. I didn't go to church, I didn't receive any phone calls- not from friends or even my family. During that week, God asked me what I would do if he didn't come home. What would I do if something happened to him? Do I

98

need him to survive? Do I need him in order to live for God? It hit me really hard. What am I doing? I didn't leave my house for a week because my husband was gone? That's not what living for Jesus looks like. All I need is God. Would I be sad if something took my husband away? Oh, heck yeah! I would be so very sad. However, God showed me what a healthy relationship looks like with my friends and my husband during that week. God showed me in scripture what I need and how He is taking care of me, but I had to seek it out. Dig into the word of God and He will speak to you. I love my husband, but I don't need him to live. Don't worry, he knows this. We have talked about this. Guess what? He doesn't need me, either. We get to be together- it's a choice, and we choose each other. I don't want any unrighteous or ungodly soul ties with anyone- including my husband. I want healthy relationships with everyone in my life. If you need someone in your life to survive, then you're not living for God; you're living for that person. That will not bring you joy; only God brings everlasting joy.

If you have an unhealthy soul tie, let me help you with the prayer to renounce it. In the name of Jesus, I renounce all spiritual soul ties to (fill in the blank) and I sever every unrighteous, unholy, ungodly soul tie that I have made. I take back anything that I have that belongs to me washed in the blood of Jesus, and I send back anything that belongs to them and I ask Jesus to sever those ties right now in Your name and connect them to Your spirit, Your truth, and Your freedom.

"As iron sharpens iron so one person sharpens another." - Proverbs 27:17

Read and Journal.
Day 1: Job 2:11
Day 2: Luke 6:31
Day 3: Proverbs 19:20
Day 4: Proverbs 22:24-25
Day 5: Proverbs 13:20
Day 6: Proverbs 27:5-6
Day 7: Proverbs 17:17
Write down one thing each day that you are thankful for.

Week 35: Obedience

Obedience is referenced in the Bible over 147 times. By definition, it's the act or practice of obeying; dutiful or submissive compliance. What does obedience look like? Obedience for some is very hard. If you have trouble with obedience, there's probably a deeper issue. Obedience to Christ brings peace. When you hear, listen, and obey Christ, you are walking in peace. If he calls you to do something, do it, even if you are scared. You can be afraid but still be courageous. There have been so many times God has called me to do or say something and to walk out obedience. There are times when I did it and times when I didn't. There have been many times God has asked me to do or say something to someone just so they know God is hearing them. He uses other people often. I have had dreams about other people and God has asked me to share the dream with them. I don't know if I'm going to sound crazy to them or if it will mean something but that's not for me to figure out. If He tells me to do it, I'm going to do it. I felt silly at first telling them, but I knew God wanted them to hear it. I have no idea if it meant anything to them, and I may never know, but I was obedient. I can attest that I was much more at peace when I was obedient. Being obedient out of love for Him outweighs my insecurities or fears.

Are there moments in your days or weeks when you need to be obedient but you aren't? Is it easy for you to follow and do everything Jesus asks of you? Do you hesitate when He calls you to speak to a stranger about what He has done for them? What does obedience look like for you? There are different types of obedience. Obedience to our parents, bosses, leaders- anyone with authority. There is always someone to show obedience toward. The world has given the word obedience such a bad reputation, but it shows honor, not weakness. The inability to obey is really what shows weakness. Obedience is an element of conduct and character. Obedience is referenced throughout scripture. In Deuteronomy 4, Moses was telling the Israelites to hear the decrees and laws. He said to follow them so that they could live and go and take possession of the land that the Lord had given them. He told them to do what was commanded and to not add or subtract from it but to keep the commandments of the Lord. Obedience was commanded in Deuteronomy 4- read it! The Lord commands this from us because He loves us.

"Obedience will always produce benefits that far outweigh the consequences of disobedience." -Priscilla Shirer

"Love the Lord your God and keep his requirements, his decrees, his laws and his commands always." -Deuteronomy 11:1

Read and Journal.
Day 1: Ephesians 6:1-3
Day 2: Corinthians 10:5
Day 3: Revelation 14:12
Day 4: Romans 1:5
Day 5: Hebrews 13:17
Day 6: John 14:15
Day 7: John 1:6

Write down one thing each day that you are thankful for.

Week 36: Feeling Hopeless & the Power of Prayer

It's time to get personal. I actually texted my oldest daughter and got permission to share this because it's her story. There is a ton of detail in this story that I may skip over just to save time but if anyone is interested or maybe going through this with someone, I will be happy to share. Feel free to email me with any questions. When my daughter was 17, she decided she was moving out because our household rules were not "working" for her. She hung out with the "wrong" people. She was drinking and using drugs. This was going on for some time. She came to a place in her life where she was very depressed and wanted help. When she was 18, she admitted herself into a mental health hospital. You would think this would be helpful, but it wasn't. She let them know she was feeling suicidal, and they put her on several different types of addictive meds (you would think as professionals they would have asked if she had a past with drugs). She was there for three weeks. Every time we went to visit her, it was like talking to and looking at a zombie. She was always so medicated you couldn't have a normal conversation with her. If anyone knows my husband, you know he went straight to those in charge. She never received one-on-one counseling, only group counseling, which doesn't work for everyone.

After many conversations, we finally got her out of

there. They sent her home with some heavy-duty narcotics which she was instructed to continue to take and go off of slowly. That isn't how it works for an addict. She continued to take them, taking more than she needed while also using other drugs and drinking. She ended up accidentally overdosing one night. Her "friends" left her there on the ground alone. I got a phone call early the next morning from a sister of one of the people who was at the party telling me we needed to come get her and that there was something wrong with her. None of her "friends" were there at this point. It was just her, on the ground, outside. They had stolen her jewelry (her purity ring we gave her) and her wallet. We picked her up and took her straight to the hospital. She was mumbling and not making any sense. They took her right away and did their thing to get the meds out of her system. The doctor told us that he couldn't even give her anything for her headache because of all that was in her system. God had His hand on her for sure.

The hospital has to report all overdoses to the state, so the state came and took her rights away. After her hospital stay, they put her back into the same mental health facility that gave her all the drugs in the first place because they wrote it off as a suicide attempt. We were not happy, and to make it even worse this was over Christmas and New Year's. So she had to spend the holidays in a mental health facility alone and away from her family. They only allow you to visit once a week. They continued to give her the same meds that she overdosed on even after we told them we did not want her on anything, but because she was 18 and the state took away her rights, they could do whatever they wanted. We were not happy. She spent three weeks there and then she came home. She was weaned off the medications right away and we just prayed and prayed. She went through some withdrawals- this was not easy to watch. We are happy to say that she is now drug-free, married, and has two babies.

That was by far the hardest thing that I've ever lived through. I felt so lonely, alone, and hopeless. I wanted to protect my child and rescue her, but I couldn't. All I had was prayer. I didn't realize at this point that prayer was so powerful. I held on to God as much as I knew how and clung to His spirit and joy. I cried daily, and I cried a lot. I love my child so much. I can't imagine how often we hurt God as we make poor choices and do what we want. Hope is vital in our walk with Christ. God is good all the time, right?

"All things work together for good to those who love God, to those who are the called according to His purpose." - Romans 8:28

"Let us then approach God's throne of grace with confidence, so that we may receive mercy and find grace to help us in our time of need." - Hebrews 4:16 NIV

"Do not conform to the pattern of this world, but be transformed by the renewing of your mind. Then you will be able to test and approve what God's will is—his good, pleasing and perfect will." - Romans 12:2 NIV

5 things I know from living this:
1. No matter the pain, God is my comfort
2. The unknown is painful but God's promise covers all.
3. Fear Is A Liar!!
4. God gave me my daughter and HE will take care of her ALWAYS
5. Pray for someone today who needs hope in what seems to be a hopeless situation.

Read and Journal.
Day 1: Proverbs 13:12
Day 2: Proverbs 4:23
Day 3: Romans 8:26-29
Day 4: 1 Thessalonians 5:8
Day 5: Jeremiah 29:11
Day 6: Hebrews 6:17-20
Day 7: 1 Peter 5:8-9

Write down one thing each day that you are thankful for.

Week 37: Poor, Naive, Scared Me

Have you ever felt that way? Hopeless? Like life isn't going as you had planned? As if you wanted it one way, and it was a good way; you thought it was God's way. You thought it would have pleased Him. I know it. I had a picture-perfect view of what my family should look like. I would be the perfect wife and have the perfect husband, the perfect daughters, the utmost perfect sons-in-law, and by far the most perfect grandchildren, dog, and cat. None of that is a true statement. None of that is perfect. I'm not perfect. I can be moody, rude, and lackadaisical. My husband isn't perfect, either; neither are my girls or my sons-in-law, and definitely not the dog (the cat is near purrfect but still sometimes bites me.)

We all have free will. Which brings me to this story. My oldest daughter has things she needs to work through with God. That's between her and God. I can't make it happen, force it to happen, or even do it for her. What can a mother do? I can choose to worry, be sad, and feel hopeless or I can choose to pray, have faith, and be hopeful. So what do I choose? It's a choice I sometimes have to make daily. The answer is both. I choose both sometimes. When doubt and fear overcome me, I'm choosing fear and hopelessness. Then God so gently reminds me that I don't need to worry, doubt, or be hopeless. Just this morning I was thinking about my oldest daughter and her husband. Praying for them and really wanting her to understand the Father's love for her. I was outside with the dog, and as I walked into the house on a shelf to the left of the door was a picture frame. In this frame, in beautiful handwriting, is a scripture that I had a friend make for her about 5 years ago. I read it and I heard God say, "I have this, she is mine and I am hers. You, mama, do not need to worry, doubt, or be fearful. This is not a hopeless situation. It's a process, and I'm helping her work through it. Take my hand and know that I am here. I know you love her, but I, her Father, love her far more than you. So trust me and continue to pray for her." The scripture, Jeremiah 31:3, reads, "I have loved you with an everlasting love." As I read that, He told me to remind her. So I will.

It's also a reminder to me that we are really not in control; we are out of control most of the time unless we are following Him. We have free will, and we can avoid and ignore God, but He's always with us, and that alone brings peace to me. I write about her struggles in a different devotional. To date, she has been clean and sober for over a year now. God is good and God is faithful but even if she didn't choose to make the right choice to get sober, I would have continued to trust Him in all things.

"The Lord appeared to us in the past, saying: "I have loved you with an everlasting love; I have drawn you with unfailing kindness." Jeremiah 31:3 NIV

Read and Journal.
Day 1: Exodus 14:14
Day 2: Isaiah 40:29
Day 3: James 4:7
Day 4: Isaiah 41:10
Day 5: 2 Chronicles 7:14
Day 6: Isaiah 40:31
Day 7: Deuteronomy 31:8

Write down one thing each day that you are thankful for.

Week 38: The Love for Grandbabies

It was July 31st, 2015. We got a phone call at about 3 am saying that it was time and that they were heading to the hospital. This story is about my oldest daughter having my first grandbaby. I had Amber on July 4, 1994. She was 8 lbs. 1 oz. and my first child. It's weird to think but now she was going to have her first baby. It was such a new experience for me as I wasn't sure what my role or my "job" was during this whole thing. Obviously as a momma, you want to go in and take over and make everything the way that it should be because that's what you do as a mom, you fix everything and you make sure that your child is okay and has all the ice chips she could possibly want but that is not my job anymore so it was an interesting experience, to say the least. I just kept praying for her, and I kept praying that I would do and say the right things. I didn't want to overstep my boundaries at all. Once I got there she wanted me right near her holding her hand and encouraging her. Her husband did an amazing job of taking care of her. She said and did some funny things as I think we all do when we're in labor, in pain, and tired of this human being inside of you.

Arianna Joy. Joy is my middle name. I was very honored that she was named after me. She was born approximately 4:30 in the afternoon on July 31, 2015. She was 7 lbs. 13 oz. and 22 inches long. My heart was overwhelmed with love. I love my daughters, but this was my granddaughter. It was a different kind of love. I still can't explain it. I just wanted to hold her and kiss her and keep her safe. Something changed in me the day she was born.

On April 10th, 2018, Jason Murphy was born, grandbaby number two. Life got a little bit better. That overwhelming love hit me again. These were moments when God showed me how much He loves us.

If we love our children and our grandchildren so very much and His love for us outdoes that by so much, just the thought of that is so amazing to me, outrageous. He has outrageous love for us. My heart overflows when I see them look at me. I want to spend all the moments that I possibly can with them. The first time Arianna called me Mimi melted me. She gives me hugs all the time, we spend time talking, and she tells me about school and what she is learning. Jason is so sweet; he always tells me that I'm beautiful and that he loves me so much. He loves calling me his girlfriend. They melt my heart.

If it's possible for me to love them as much as I do from the first moment that I saw them, then think about how much more our heavenly Father loves us. Watching them grow up, watching them go through different stages in life, learning words, learning to count, learning ABCs, learning to speak a different language, learning how to put sentences together and having them make sense. The pride that I have when it comes to them, how proud I am of them, is just a small, small reflection of how God looks at us, cares for us, loves us, and wants the best for us. That's why he disciplines us. It's just this crazy love that I have for both of them. Like even when they're getting into something or doing something they're not supposed to be doing, I can't help but look at them and see their little faces and big blue eyes look back at me and think they are perfect. God sees us the same way. His love is overflowing and overwhelming and outrageous. It's so good. Nothing is better, nothing!!! You guys think about it, He sent His only son, Jesus to this earth to die on a cross for our sins because He loves us enough that He wants to spend eternity with us. That is the Good News!! The Gospel!! Wouldn't you die for someone that you love? I would die for them, I would die to protect them, I would do everything that it took to keep them safe, to give them everlasting life. That's what God did. John 3:16-18 says, "For God so loved the world that he gave his one and only son, that whosoever believes in him shall not perish but have eternal life. For God did not send his son into the world to condemn the world, but to save the world through him. Whoever believes in him is not condemned, but whoever does not believe stands condemned already because they have not believed in the name of God's one and only son."

He loves us, He died for us, He tells us that He's here to save the world through Him and then He warns us that if we don't believe in Him, we are not following Him, then we stand condemned because we don't believe. He is a good loving God; He is not a bad God. He is love.

Read and Journal.
Day 1: John 3:15
Day 2: John 3:16
Day 3: John 3:17
Day 4: John 3:18
Day 5: John 3:19
Day 6: John 3:20
Day 7: John 3:21

Write down one thing each day that you are thankful for.

Week 39: Wisdom

The Bible says to get wisdom at all cost. All cost! I have a hard time thinking that it is not a big deal when it's written like that. Proverbs 4 talks about paying attention to this teaching to get wisdom and understanding and to take hold of these words and guard your heart. The beginning of wisdom is getting wisdom. Do not forsake wisdom. Wisdom will give you a garland to grace your head and give you a glorious crown. What do you think that means? The path of the righteous is like the morning sun. Shining ever brighter till the light of day. But the way of the wicked is like deep darkness; they do not know what makes them stumble. Proverbs 4:18-19 I don't have some cool story about my life where God granted me an abundance of wisdom. I wish that was the case. I do however pray for wisdom, want and seek it. After I met Jesus and was saved by his grace, I started reading his word to learn all I could. We want wisdom to know what to do, what choices and decisions to make and we sometimes make ourselves sick and paralyze ourselves just from the thought of making the wrong decision.

Listen to this story: "At Gibeon, the Lord appeared to Solomon in a dream by night, and God said, 'Ask what I shall give you.' And Solomon said, 'You have shown great and steadfast love to your servant David my father, because he walked before you in faithfulness, in righteousness, and in uprightness of heart toward you. And you have kept for him this great and steadfast love and have given him a son to sit on his throne this day. And now, O Lord my God, you have made your servant king in place of David my father, although I am but a little child. I do not know how to go out or come in. And your servant is in the midst of your people whom you have chosen, a great people, too many to be numbered or counted for multitude. Give your servant therefore an understanding mind to govern your people, that I may discern between good and evil, for who is able to govern this your great people?' It pleased the Lord that Solomon had asked this. And God said to him, 'Because you have asked this, and have not asked for yourself long life or riches or the life of your enemies, but have asked for yourself understanding to discern what is right, behold, I now do according to your word. Behold, I give you a wise and discerning mind, so that none like you has been before you and none like you shall arise after you. I give you also what you have not asked, both riches and honor, so that no other king shall compare with you, all your days. And if you will walk in my ways, keeping my statutes and my commandments, as your father David walked, then I will lengthen your days.'" - 1 Kings 3:5-14 ESV

I have been praying for wisdom since I read that story in scripture. God has given me the gift of discernment and he shows me things all the time. He loves us so much that He tells me things to give someone an encouraging word or pray specifically for someone. God gives us gifts to advance his Kingdom. All you need to do is ask. He wants to give you wisdom. Wisdom keeps your paths straight. Wisdom keeps you out of trouble. Wisdom helps you to make a choice. Wisdom shows you who to fully trust and who not to. So have faith, do not be afraid of tomorrow or of what may come. Do not fear making the wrong decision, what college to attend, what job offer to take, who to marry. If you are walking with God, your choice will be blessed because God is in the center of it. Just make a decision!! Matthew 6:34 says "Therefore do not worry about tomorrow, for tomorrow will worry about itself. Each day has enough trouble of its own." We need to be the confident people God intended for us to be. Stop living afraid!!

Read and Journal.
Day 1:1 Kings 3
Day 2: 1 Kings 3:1-4
Day 3: 1 Kings 3:5-9
Day 4: 1 Kings 3:10-15

Day 5: 1 Kings 3:16-28
Day 6: Psalms 37:30
Day 7: Psalms 111:10

Write down one thing each day that you are thankful for.

Week 40: Worship

When I think of worship, I often think of the words of the song "So Will I" by Hillsong United. You'll need to look it up but I love the verse that says, "In the vapor of your breath the planets formed | If the stars were made to worship so will I." Then it goes on to say, "If creation sings Your praises, so will I | If the stars were made to worship, so will I | If the mountains bow in reverence, so will I | If the oceans roar Your greatness, so will I | For if everything exists to lift You high, so will I." Just imagine that. Sit in His presence and soak that in. Wow- if the stars were made to worship, so will I- just wow!! Music is so powerful- that's why it's so important to me to be mindful of the music we listen to.

When I was younger, I listened to 70's and 80s rock. Motley Crüe, Metallic, Rat, Cinderella, Ozzy. Any hair band would do. I did not have an understanding of what it was doing to me spiritually. When I became a Christian and worship music was introduced to me, I was blown away by how it made me feel. Every time I would listen to it I would cry and feel so safe, calm, and at peace with everything. Even when everything may have not been great, I felt at peace. In those moments of worship, it was so great. So many times prayer is answered while worshiping God. When we declare things over us and pray to God, something happens and things change. I play worship music as much as I can in my home. I'm playing it now as I write this devotional. I want a home filled with worship. I want life spoken over my home, my husband, myself, my children, and my grandchildren. When we worship, heaven invades earth, the enemy is defeated, chains fall off, and negative things that have been spoken over us are broken off. Claim it, speak it, believe it!!

There are different ways to worship as well. You can worship with music, you can worship God by doing the very best that you can at your everyday job. You can worship while doing the laundry or washing the dishes or parenting (I suggest worshiping while parenting) or being a good wife or being a good husband- the list goes on and on. You can worship in everything that you do. David was dancing (worship) before the Lord with all of his might. Michal saw from the window and she despised him in her heart because of what she saw. After David celebrated, he went home. Michal said some not so nice things to him, sarcastically saying how the king of Israel has distinguished himself today, going around half naked in full view of slave girls and servants as any vulgar fellow would. David said it was before the Lord who chose me rather than your father to rule over the Lord's people Israel. David was not going to allow her to make him feel bad for worshiping God. David said, "I will celebrate before the Lord. I will become even more undignified than this and I will be humiliated in my own eyes but by the slave girls I will be held in honor." Don't allow someone, no matter who they are, to stop your worship. Worship with all your heart. Become undignified before the Lord. Proclaim worship over yourselves daily.

Read and Journal.
Day 1: What takeaway have you gotten from today's Scripture? What are your thoughts on worship?
Day 2: 1 Chronicles 16:23-31 What is God saying?
Day 3: Daniel 2:20. Why do you think Daniel is giving God praise?
Day 4: Deuteronomy 10:21
Day 5: Jeremiah 20:13
Day 6: Psalm 75:1
Day 7: Take today and journal what God has shown you about worship. Prayer: *Lord, I thank you so much for being able to freely praise You. You deserve all praise and worship. Your love, mercy, peace, and kindness follow me always. You are always there for me. Show me how to truly worship You in all I do, every day of my life. I love You. Amen.*

Write down one thing each day that you are thankful for.

Week 41: Finances

I've always listened to those who are wise with their finances. One thing I wish I learned when I was younger was to never get a credit card. Credit card debt has gotten me in trouble as far as not having money to bless people because I have a debt that must be paid monthly. I do realize there are some people who know how to handle their finances and use credit cards correctly. I, however, am still learning. My husband and I want to be good stewards over our finances. We want to be debt-free and we want to be in a place to bless people. It's my very favorite thing to do. I pray for wisdom so I know how to become debt-free. We have closed all of our card accounts we had opened, and we are getting there. These are mistakes we made early in our marriage that we are still paying for. I want financial freedom use what I have God's way. We have a rental house we've tried selling- it didn't sell. A friend of ours who is very good with his finances said to keep it because it makes us money. We attempted to refinance the home we bought two years ago but were told there wasn't enough equity yet. I prayed it would be God's will and for Him to shut doors that aren't ours to walk through. So I am content. I will continue to listen to what He is calling us to do. He knows far more than I. His will, not mine. We got a call saying we could refinance. Our rate is lower than it was before! We paid off credit card debt and our house payment is slightly lower than it was before this and we will still be able to pay the house off in less than 15 years. I believe God saw our hearts and blessed this.

Money can drive a man in a good way or a bad way- it depends on your heart. The love of money is the root of all kinds of evil. Some people live to just make money and focus so much on money that they have forgotten about God, and in doing this have brought on much grief to themselves. I don't want money to dictate my life, I want my life to dictate my money. There are so many avenues of finances. Be wise and don't allow money and greed to control your every move. Jesus calls us to be humble and to be humble in our finances as well. Give what God tells you to give. There was a woman who gave all she had. She understood the kindness of God. She understood His promises to take care of us.

"Jesus sat down opposite the place where the offerings were put in and watched the crowd putting their money into the temple treasury. Many rich people threw in large amounts. But a poor widow came and put in two very small copper coins, worth only a few cents. Calling his disciples to him, Jesus said, truly I tell you, this poor widow has put more into the treasury than all the others. They all gave out of their wealth; but she, out of her poverty, put in everything - all she had to live on." Mark 12:41-44

"For where your treasure is, there your heart will be also." Matthew 6:21

1. Have you ever taken a finance class? If not, check out Dave Ramsey.
2. Do you have and follow a budget? If not, make one!!
3. Make sure you are tithing and have a savings account. Both are so important.
4. If you are good in this area, help someone else become good in this area as well.
5. Pray for someone who needs financial freedom and reach out to them with encouragement.

Read and Journal.
Day 1- Ecclesiastes 5:10
Day 2: Romans 13:8
Day 3: Psalm 37:16-17
Day 4: Proverbs 13:11
Day 5: Hebrews 13:5
Day 6: Matthew 19:21
Day 7: Matthew 6:24

Write down one thing each day that you are thankful for.

*From the time I wrote this devotional to publication we are officially debt-free due to tools we learned from Dave Ramsey.

Week 42: Purpose

What is my purpose in life? I also think of it as the assignment that God has given me. We all want it, we all want to belong and have meaning. I know I have a purpose, I always have. Sometimes, purpose dies in the midst of our insecurities. We need to fight it. I believe my purpose has changed over the years and that's okay. When I was younger my purpose was to be a kid, to learn and to grow and gain wisdom. As I got older my purpose changed. I got married and became a mom. My purpose was to be a good wife and an amazing mom. To teach my girls what it looks like to be a godly mother, woman, friend, and wife. In 2000 my husband and I started working with youth students and my purpose changed a little. Now I added leader and mentor to that list. Being a good example to students, showing love, listening, showing compassion, and guiding them through life. This was my purpose, also known as my assignment for about 18 years. Raising my girls, getting them through middle and high school. It had a great purpose. I was blessed that God gave me that purpose. After 18 years of leading students, my husband and I transferred into a new position at our church. He is currently an associate pastor along with the men's ministry and heading up the ministry academy. That was his purpose; what was mine? I could ask that question without fear. I know my identity so I'm not afraid of the future. What is my purpose/assignment now? I'm helping with the ministry academy, ministering, and leading young adults. I mentor young adult men and women. I also mentor older folks than me when God puts that opportunity in my path. I get stay home most days and help raise my grandbabies and help my daughter as she is in the process of going back to college. I'm just making myself available to what God has for me.

What's your purpose? What is your assignment? Make yourself available and then let God do the rest. Our purpose is his purpose. We need to show who God is in all we do and say.

"'For I know the plans I have for you,' declares the Lord. 'plans to prosper you and not to harm you, plans to give you hope and a future. Then you were calling me and come and pray to me, and I will listen to you. You will seek me and find me when you seek me with all your heart.'" - Jeremiah 29:11:13

"But I have raised you up for this very purpose, that I might show you my power and that my name might be proclaimed in all the earth." - Exodus 9:16

Read and Journal.
Day 1: Journal about today's devotional and scripture reading
Day 2: 2 Corinthians 8:21
Day 3: Ephesians 1:11
Day 4:1 Peter 1:2
Day 5: Psalms 57:2
Day 6: Isaiah 26:3:4
Day 7: Reflect on this last week and journal about the purpose in your life and the steps are going to take to get there.

Write down one thing each day that you are thankful for.

Week 43: I'm "Just" a Mom

Do you ever question your purpose? Has anyone ever said something to you that was so simple yet so profound that it literally changed your outlook on something? It was in this moment that it penetrated my heart so deeply that everything within my heart and mind was being rewired by one simple affirmation and statement. What was that statement you ask? I'll get to that in a moment. I know many people but I don't know many highly intelligent, intellectual, straight-to-the-point, say-it-with-conviction and confidence, not-going-to-beat-around-the-bush kind of people. This man who spoke life over me is a president of a bible college, one of the smartest people I have ever met. A "think outside the box" man who loves Jesus and his family and it shows. Needless to say, I respect this man. We were in a conversation and he asked me what I do. I responded with "I'm just a mom." Without hesitation, he looked directly into my eyes and said, "Don't ever say 'just.' You are a mom, and what you do is important, you are doing things other people aren't. Don't ever say 'just.'" It was a simple truth that God used to change my outlook on what He has given me and why.

Have you ever noticed how in Disney movies the princesses don't have mothers? That has always been a mystery to me. Moms are important. As far back as I can remember, I've always wanted to be a mom. I wasn't like other little girls who wanted to be a singer, model, a vet, zoologist, microbiologist, or any other "gist" I just wanted to be a mom. I became a mom in 1994; that was the greatest day of my life, besides, of course, marrying my husband. In 1998 I became mom to daughter number two. Then we started to get involved in church and the youth group, and as relationships grew, I became "mom" to many. Getting involved in 2000 with youth was a dream and I was content in this for a very long time.

We transitioned from youth in February of 2019. It wasn't until then that the enemy started whispering lies to me about this. His lies say, "You are just a mom," "You have nothing to offer now," "You are not making a difference," "No one sees value in you," and "Your words are empty and meaningless" so I started really noticing what others around me are doing. Comparison was setting in and so was bitterness. I saw people so talented on stage singing and playing instruments, people who were speaking and teaching with such confidence, people who were taking amazing pictures, those who were so good at social media, the list goes on. I don't do any of that and honestly, none of that was or is my heart. I would hear the enemy say it again, "You're just a mom." Now, the verdict is still out on my mothering skills, but I love my girls and I've kept them alive this long, they love Jesus and have beautiful hearts, so mothering them wasn't bothering me. What was bothering me was that I didn't think I had value in the church or was worthy of being on staff with such talented people. I'm just a mom after all. I have no title. I tried doing different things like speaking (no thanks, I'll leave that to those that are called), taking pictures, helping with social media, helping in other ministries, which is normally good... unless that is not the assignment God has asked of you. I wanted to be "more," more than just a mom. Any female can be a mom, that's not special. I wanted to be valued and special.

The whole time God was and is calling me to be a mom to the FCA students and I was mad about it. I was mad that my name on our staff chat was "FCA Mom." I felt devalued and unimportant. Wow, I was a pathetic mess and so blinded by lies!! I kept praying that God would show me my value, and within a time period of two weeks, we received four different text testimonies from prior youth students and leaders who served with us. These texts talked about what our consistency in their lives did for them. Two of them asked for us to meet their person of interest for our "approval" and the other two were "thank you" for being faithful and consistent in their lives and our walk with Jesus. I heard God say to me, "You are a faithful mom to them, and that's what I called you to be. Your assignment is to be a mom to many." That changed my attitude real quick. I love that I get to be the FCA Mom. I wouldn't want it any other way. I no longer question my purpose or place. I'm no longer searching for or wanting to be anything other than what I am. I'm not "just" a mom, I am the best mom, I am the mom they ask questions to, I am the mom they want advice from, I am the mom they ask prayer from, I am the mom they want hugs from, I am the cool mom (joking about the last one of course). God has shown me how important it is to have my title and I wear it proudly. Not everyone gets to hold this title, whether it be for their birth children or the ones He brings to you. I have little and older sisters in the faith that I mom and didn't even realize it. He's given me something I didn't even know I had because I was too busy wanting what others had. Let me say that again because it is too good to quickly read over. He's given me something I didn't even know I had because I was too busy wanting what others had. I am thankful I didn't stay in this place too long and that I'm a quicker learner now than I used to be.

Proverbs 31:28 & 30 - "28 Her children arise and call her blessed; her husband also, and he praises her. 30 Charm is deceptive, and beauty is fleeting; but a woman who fears the LORD is to be praised.

Read and Journal.
Day 1: Deuteronomy 6:5-9
Day 2: Psalms 127:3
Day 3: Proverbs 22:6
Day 4: Titus 2:5
Day 5: Proverbs 31:17
Day 6: Jeremiah 1:5
Day 7: Proverbs 31:15

Write down one thing each day that you are thankful for.

Week 44: Faith & Courage

As I've been reading Esther, I have been praying for faith and courage. I've been on a journey for about 3 months that doesn't have to do with anyone else except me, God, and the book of Esther. I've been praying for faith and courage in the ministries of the church, the leaders, staff, for those who enter the church who may have given their life to Christ before or maybe never before, but that all in these positions would walk in faith and courage. You may or may not know me, but if you do, you know that the microphone is not my favorite friend. Why, you ask? Because when I speak into it my voice becomes louder, and the entire room can hear me. That is terrifying. What if I stutter? What if I stumble or get choked up, what if I forget what I'm saying, what if I sound stupid? What if, what if, what if. I was asked to run prayer one Sunday morning- a simple task. You grab the mic, you share what's on your heart, and you break up into your prayer groups. It's not that hard, right? Then why did my heart race a million miles an hour when I was asked to do it? Fear is the opposite of courage, and doubt the opposite of faith. I have been reading Esther for the last three months, and the first thing that came to my mind was not faith or courage, it was doubt and fear. To be completely honest, if anyone else had asked me, I probably would have said no, but because it was my friend Dena, I said yes. I said yes to her because I knew that if she believed in me, then I should be able to believe in me. It was a reminder that God believes in me. So I said yes. I thought to myself, "What in the world could I possibly share? Maybe I'll just welcome everybody and break them off into their prayer circles and not share anything." God had a different plan. It was like He tapped me on the shoulder and reminded me of what I had been reading for the last three months. Right... I hear you Lord, and I will listen. So I shared what I have been learning about Esther

123

and about how we are supposed to walk in our everyday lives. (If you haven't read the book of Esther, you should go do that now.)

After Mordecai found out what Haman's plan was for the Jews, Mordecai asked Esther to go before the King to beg him to save the Jewish people. She could die doing this. One does not just mosey on into the Royal Palace and say, "Hey King, husband guy, I have a favor to ask of you." She knew that she could die. So she sent a messenger back to Mordecai explaining that. He responded by saying, "Esther, who knows but that you have come to your royal position for such a time as this?" I believe in that moment that faith and courage rose up in Esther, and her response was, "If I perish, I perish." Let's be obedient to what God is calling us to do, and if we fail, we fail; if we fall, we fall; if we perish, we perish; but we are doing what God has called us to do. Let's be like Esther and live in faith and courage; we were made for such a time as this!!!

"For if you remain silent at this time, relief and deliverance for the Jews will arise from another place, but you and your father's family will perish. And who knows but that you have come to your royal position for such a time as this?" - Esther 4:14, NIV

When we went to Idaho with FCMA a few years back, God gave a friend of mine, Adam Cooke a word for me, and I recently came across it after all of this had happened. It was simple, and this is what it was: Esther 5:1-8 - God says you are a Queen and wear a great crown. I will receive that!!

Action steps:
Day 1: Today, journal what your takeaway was from Esther's story.
Day 2: Esther 2:15-17- Esther finds favor with the king, and he chooses her to be Queen. Do you think God has favor on your life? Why or why not? Think, meditate on it, and make a list/journal.
Day 3: Esther 2:15-17- refer back to yesterday's journaling. Thank God for the areas in which you have favor. Make a list of the areas that you have faith and courage in or areas you want faith and courage. Thank God in advance for those areas. Journal.

Day 4: Esther 4:14- part of this scripture says, "'And who knows but that you have come to your royal position for such a time as this?'" Have you ever had a moment like this? Where God has called you to do something you felt scared or unsure to do? Journal about it.

Day 5: Esther 5:1- "On the third day, Esther put on her royal robes and stood in the inner court of the palace, in front of the king's hall. The king was sitting on his royal throne in the hall, facing the entrance." Esther entered in not knowing if she was going to die. With much faith and courage, she did it. Ever have a moment like this? Journal.

Day 6: Take today's time of devotion and put on your favorite worship song and ask God to reveal to you what your "such a time as this" is. Journal.

Day 7: Journal and reflect on the last six days and what God has shown you about yourself about faith and courage. Lord, thank you so much for taking me on this journey of faith and courage. If you call me to it, I will do it. Even if I'm scared, I will do it. If I fail, I fail, if I fall, I fall, and if I perish, I perish, but I will do it willingly because I know you love me and have my best interest in mind. I love you. Amen.

Write down one thing each day that you are thankful for.

Week 45: Joy

At the end of the verse in Nehemiah 8:10 it says, "For the joy of the Lord is your strength." Psalms 28:7 says, "the Lord is my strength and shield. I trust Him with all my heart; He helps me, and my heart is filled with joy. I burst out in songs of Thanksgiving." James 1:2-3 says to "consider it pure joy when we face trials of many kinds because the testing of our faith produces perseverance." Scriptures about joy are throughout the Bible. Proverbs 10:28, Psalms 47:1, Isaiah 9:3, 1 Peter 1:8-9, Romans 15:13, John 1:12,. There are many other scriptures about joy, but the writer isn't sitting on a beach in Hawaii. He's sitting in a jail cell that looks more like a hole in the ground than what you'd think of as a jail cell today. This cell is dirt and rock, no toilet, no clean water, and yet he writes about how good God is and truly and sincerely cares about people enough to write God-given scripture for us to read today. That is pure JOY. Look at Paul. He looks past his own circumstances for the sake of others. He urges the Philippians to have a servant's heart and attitude just like Jesus had. Jesus did not grasp his high position but humbled himself even to the point of death, all for the sake of others.

When I think of joy, I think of things like laying on the beach in the sun with a sweet tea and the sound of my kids and grandbabies playing or a newborn's very first cry after childbirth or a loved one's wedding day or your favorite meal after fasting or even a puppy. We don't think of joy coming from a prison cell with dirt walls. Thank you, Paul, for your example of joy in your hard times. Thank you for sitting there and thinking of others as you looked around and all you saw was rock and dirt and darkness. I went to Rome on a mission trip a while back and I visited the prison cell where Paul sat and wrote Philippians. It was heartbreaking, and it changed the way that I read scripture. This book was not written in great circumstances, it was cold and musty and it smelled weird, and I got claustrophobic and had to leave the room. I couldn't imagine being in prison there. I couldn't imagine being joyful to the point of writing these letters so that we could many, many, many years later read them and have hope. Joy cannot be taken away because it has been given by God. Happiness is circumstantial, but joy is everlasting. You could have joy in the midst of the hardest thing you've ever had to face. If you have God, you literally have joy.

But what does it matter? The important thing is that in every way, whether from false motives or true, Christ is preached. And because of this, I rejoice. Yes, and I will continue to rejoice, for I know that through your prayers and God's provision of the Holy Spirit of Jesus Christ, what has happened to me will turn out for my deliverance. I eagerly expect and hope that I will in no way be ashamed, but will have sufficient courage so that now, as always, Christ will be exalted in my body, whether by life or by death. For to me, to live is Christ and to die is gain. If I am to go on living in the body, this will mean fruitful labor for me. Yet what shall I choose? I do not know! I am torn between the two: I desire to depart and be with Christ, which is better by far; but is it more necessary for you that I remain in the body. Convinced of this, I know that I will remain, and I will continue with all of you for your progress and joy in the faith, so that through my being with you again you're both staying in Jesus Christ will abound on the account of me. Philippians 1:18-26 WOW!! The words "joy" and "rejoice" are found over 10 times in Philippians.

Read and Journal.
Day 1: What brings you joy? How do you describe it? Journal.
Day 2: Philippians 1
Day 3: Philippians 2
Day 4: Philippians 3
Day 5: Philippians 4
Day 6: Philippians was written while Paul was in prison in Rome. What can you do on a daily basis to have the same outlook on life as Paul? Journal

Day 7: Philippians 2:14-18 - List some ways to live this daily.

Write down one thing each day that you are thankful for.

Week 46: Rome or Bust

Fear can be so crippling. It's paralyzing. It literally stops us from pushing forward. It holds us back from accomplishing things God placed on our hearts. Fear lies to us about who we are, what we can do, and how others see us. Fear is a lie, and lies are the enemy's native tongue. Before you can fight fear, you have to first recognize that fear is a battle for you. Fear has held me back in many areas. Fear has told me that my ideas are small and meaningless. Fear has told me that I'm not a good wife, mom, or friend. Fear whispers in my ear and convinces me to doubt myself. It tries to erase the truth that God speaks over me, over my life, and over my family. Once you know fear is the thing that is holding you back from making new friends, taking that job, joining that ministry, or pursuing your dreams, you have the key to fighting that fear. Ever hear the saying "it's a battlefield of the mind"? It is!! It's a battle within yourself. Daily we need the Armor of God.

I had the opportunity of going on a missions trip with my daughter to Rome, Italy, and fear almost stopped me. My husband was not going and that was scary to me. I had never traveled out of the U.S. without him. He took care of everything- who's going to hold the money, who's going to tell us where we're going to eat, who's going to help me cross the road, who's going to keep me from getting hit by a car as I cross the road? Seriously, these were the things I was thinking of!! Who is going to sit next to me on the plane, what if Kelli doesn't get to sit next to me on the plane? Who's going to keep me from having a nervous breakdown on the plane? I can not go to Rome without my husband. That's it. I'm not going. I was well prepared to tell my daughter and Pastor Carl that I was not going to Rome. It was in this very moment that the Lord told me I was going to go tell Faye, who is Pastor Carl's wife that I was going to Rome and that she was to hold me accountable to it. Why did God pick her? If you know her then you know exactly why God picked her. If you don't know her, let me just tell you a little bit about Faye. She is the kindest, sweetest, most loving friend I know. She also doesn't accept your excuses and demands your best- always. So I knew exactly why God chose her. I had a choice to make. I could choose to tell her what God wanted me to tell her or I could keep it to myself and simply not go. I want the most God has for me, so I was determined to push past myself and I told Faye the battle I was having within myself. I literally felt sick to my stomach as I was talking to her, but I knew it was the right thing to do. Long story short, this Rome missions trip was the greatest missions trip that I had ever been on. Not because I was in Rome, but because I pushed past myself and I did something on my own, with God.

Do not allow fear to dictate your path!! The enemy knew I was going to grow and he did not want me to, so he was trying to place fear within my heart to keep me isolated. BAM!!! In your face, Satan!!

"Finally, be strong in the Lord and in his mighty power. Put on the full armor of God, so that you can take your stand against the devil's schemes. For our struggle is not against flesh and blood, but against the rulers, against the authorities, against the powers of this dark world and against the spiritual forces of evil in the heavenly realms. Therefore put on the full armor of God, so that when the day of evil comes, you may be able to stand your ground, and after you have done everything, to stand. Stand firm then, with the belt of truth buckled around your waist, with the breastplate of righteousness in place, and with your feet fitted with the readiness that comes from the gospel of peace. In addition to all this, take up the shield of faith, with which you can extinguish all the flaming arrows of the evil one. Take the helmet of salvation and the sword of the Spirit, which is the word of God. And pray in the Spirit on all occasions with all kinds of prayers and requests. With this in mind, be alert and always keep on praying for all the Lord's people." - Ephesians 6:10-18 NIV

"He will never leave you nor forsake you. Do not be afraid; do not be discouraged." - Deuteronomy 31:8

I like to imagine God saying this, just to me, as He looks me in the eyes and holds my face in His hands. "I am with you. I am your protector and your biggest fan." Paul and Timothy remind us in Philippians, "Being confident of this, that he who began a good work in you will carry it on to completion until the day of Christ Jesus." Philippians 1:6 NIV.

To fight fear, we need to counteract it with God's peace. We need to know what the word says. We need to know what God says about us. Start speaking truth over yourself. Do this every single day. Let me say that again. Speak God's word over yourself every. Single. Day. Do it as many times in a day as you need to. Your heart needs to be penetrated by His truth. Take every thought captive and rebuke fear. Don't let it take hold of your heart and build its home there. Fear is an unwanted guest. Fear is a liar!!

"We demolish arguments and every pretension that sets itself up against the knowledge of God, and we take captive every thought to make it obedient to Christ." -2 Corinthians 10:5 NIV

1. Write about a time fear stopped you from doing something
2. Write about a time you conquered fear. What helped you?
3. What advice would you tell others on how to defeat fear?
4. List one thing you will do differently to counteract fear.
5. Pray for someone you know that's fighting fear and give them an encouraging word today.

Read and Journal.
Day 1: Psalm 27:1
Day 2: Psalm 55:22
Day 3: Deuteronomy 31:6
Day 4: Isaiah 41:13-14
Day 5: Psalm 46:1
Day 6: Psalm 118:6-7
Day 7: Proverbs 29:25
Write down one thing each day that you are thankful for.

Week 47: Love

"No, in all these things we are more than conquerors through him who loved us. For I am convinced that neither death nor life, neither angels nor demons, neither the present nor the future, nor any powers, neither height nor depth, nor anything else in all creation, will be able to separate us from the love of God that is in Jesus Christ our Lord." - Romans 8:37-39

Wow. He really loves us!! I know there are all kinds of different versions of the Bible out there but I use the NIV. The word love is referenced 538 times in the NIV. Sin is referenced 400 times. Sin is important to talk about, but love is mentioned so many more times than the sin that we fall into. Have you ever heard of the love chapter in the Bible? I have always heard 1 Corinthians 13 referred to as the love chapter. Now if you stop to think about the things that you love or the people that you love, different thoughts and different people come to mind. But if we really line it up with what the Bible says love is, are we really loving people? Let me tell you what 1 Corinthians 13:4-8 says. Buckle up, some of you may have to sit down for this. (I'm only half kidding, but really.) "Love is patient, love is kind. It does not envy, it does not boast, it is not proud. It does not dishonor others, it is not self-seeking, it is not easily angered, it keeps no record of wrongs. Love does not delight in evil but rejoices with the truth. It always protects, always trusts, always hopes, always perseveres. Love never fails!!"

To be completely honest I do not remember the exact moment when I fell in love with my husband. I think it was little things throughout our relationship that added up and then one day it was just a realization that I was in love with him and he was different than anyone else that I knew. He was the nicest person that I had ever met. I remember telling him that he was my best friend and the nicest guy that I knew. As I learned more about the Lord I soon realized that what I loved about my husband was the love of the Lord. He was being Christlike and that was what I loved. Now the love for my daughters was an instant love. I loved them at the moment I was pregnant and that feeling really came to me when I gave birth to them. The moment I looked into their eyes and held them for the very first time I knew I loved them and I would protect them till the end of my days. But when I line them up with what's in this chapter, I'm not always truly loving them. It's something that I reflect on often because I want to love them the way God is asking me to love them. I love my girls more than anything. Love is patient, and love is kind. I'm not always patient, and I'm not always kind with them. It does not envy, it does not boast; it is not proud, and it does not dishonor others. It is not self-seeking, and it is not easily angered, it keeps no record of wrongs. Well, some of those that are listed I do well at; others I do not. Sometimes, I'm easily angered. Sometimes, I will remember the wrong that was done. I am not loving them the way God is asking me to love them. Love does not delight in evil but rejoices with the truth. I think I have that one down, I hope I do. It always protects, yes? yes!! I will always protect them. I have hope that I am doing that well. It always trusts. I don't always trust them, but I need to. It always hopes and always perseveres. I think I have the hope and the perseverance down for my girls. Love never fails. I love them unconditionally. I just need to do a better job at it. If you ask them, I'm sure they would say that I love them very well, but according to what Scripture says, I've got some work to do, and I'm willing to do it.

Over this next week, we're going to break down 1 Corinthians 13, and we are going to apply these in our daily lives.

Read and Journal.
Day 1:1 Corinthians 13
Day 2:1 Corinthians 4
Day 3:1 Corinthians 5
Day 4: 1 Corinthians 6
Day 5:1 Corinthians 7

Day 6:1 Corinthians 8

Day 7: Over the last six days, we have been applying and reading 1 Corinthians 13. What have you learned in the last week, and what has changed in reference to the way you love people? Journal.

Write down one thing each day that you are thankful for.

Week 48: Mercy, Over and Over and Over Again

Forgiveness involves the overcoming of anger and resentment, and mercy involves the withholding of harsh treatment that one has a right to inflict but what does the Bible say about forgiveness? "Bear with each other and forgive one another if any of you has a grievance against someone. Forgive as the Lord forgave you." - Colossians 3:13. We are called to forgive each other; we all do things that need forgiveness. Withholding forgiveness from someone is like drinking poison and expecting the other person to die. We are hurting ourselves if we hold on to hurt and bitterness. I totally understand that some wounds are deep and personal. I know, I've lived it over and over and over again. I don't want to withhold forgiveness or love from anyone, not even those who have hurt me. I have stories that would justify unforgiveness in a worldly outlook, but we aren't called to have that view. I climb higher so I can see clearer. I will choose to forgive, and forgive, and forgive again if needed.

That doesn't mean that we become a punching bag for people. There are boundaries that need to take place, trust that needs to be rebuilt, and in some cases, relationships that need to be reconciled. Forgiving is the goal. I like to think of my mind as a palace and I am the queen of that palace. I am responsible for what goes on in the palace and who is allowed to enter. I am the overseer of my mind palace. I refuse to allow the enemy or the enemy's tricks to make my palace its home. They sometimes sneak in, but I'm always cleaning the palace, as we all should. If you are not on high alert for what's entering your palace the place will get messy real fast.

Forgiving people who hurt you, hurt those you love, did awful things to those you don't know, it doesn't matter what it is, we are called to forgive. I have been wronged and lied about, I know people who have killed loved ones, tortured and murdered an innocent child, people who have stolen from loved ones, liars, cheaters, abusers, the list goes on. We need to forgive and pray for them because God loves them and wants better for them. We can't always stop evil from coming but we can do what God teaches us to do. I forgive those who have done wrong against me, I forgive those who have hurt my loved ones, I forgive those who have lied and cheated me. I choose to forgive and so can you. Lay it at His feet; it's not your fight to fight. To have mercy and forgive is what God wants from us.

"The Lord our God is merciful and forgiving, even though we have rebelled against him;" - Daniel 9:9

If the King of Kings can forgive us for all of our rebellion then we should be able to forgive those who wrong us.

1. To have mercy on someone and forgive is Christ-like, do you regularly practice this? Why or why not?
2. Is there someone in your life you need to have mercy on and forgive? Who? Release them, ask for forgiveness for holding on to it, and forgive them.
3. What is one thing you will do differently tomorrow to be more like Jesus?
4. Journal about a time someone forgave you and how it made you feel.
5. Pray for a friend or family member who needs to forgive, and give them encouragement in this.

Read and Journal.

Day 1: Matthew 6:14-15
Day 2: Luke 17:3-4
Day 3: Ephesians 4:31-32
Day 4: 1 John 1:9
Day 5: Ephesians 1:7

Day 6: Numbers 14:19-21
Day 7: Micah 7:18-19

Write down one thing each day that you are thankful for.

Week 49: Marriage

I am by no means an expert on marriage. What I do know I'll share with you. When I got married I was 20, my husband was 18, and I was 4 months pregnant. No, we didn't get married because I was pregnant; we sincerely loved each other. These are the things I know; I hope you have a notepad and I hope you're taking notes. Please learn from my mistakes.

I know that God must be the center of your marriage or it's going to be really hard, and it's really hard to begin with. I can't imagine marriage without God. (If you're not married yet please don't let that statement scare you.)

I know that giving up is not an option. Marriage is important and not to be taken lightly. It is not a piece of paper. It's not something to just do because it seems fun. Marriage is a commitment and needs to be taken seriously.

I know that you need to put your spouse's cares and concerns before your own. This is a two-way street. However, if you get this before your spouse, do it anyway.

I know it's helpful to get pre-marriage counseling before marriage, and if you are already married and never did this, do it.

I know it's good to get marriage counseling because believe it or not, you are not an expert on your spouse, and I'll go as far as saying there is probably a thing or two you could learn about yourself.

I know that pushing through the hard times is a must. God is a must! My husband and I have been married for over 28 years. We married in 1994. We have been through many things over the years we always pushed through. We've been to marriage counseling, have had very long talks, raised children, raised other people's children, the list goes on and on.

We have many friends and acquaintances who have given up and divorced. It's so sad to me. I don't know what their relationship is with God or what it's like now, but I know how to make a marriage work. Ready for the answer? This could change your marriage. It's a choice, not a feeling. Let me say that again- it is a choice, not a feeling. Jason and I have an amazing marriage, and we choose to love each other each and every day. Both my husband and I have put God before each other. I know that may sound foreign to some, but without God as your very first love, how can you possibly love someone else? I don't need my husband to survive and he doesn't need me, either, but I choose to be with him as he chooses to be with me. It takes two willing people to make a marriage work. *Lord may my children see a marriage worth imitating when they look at our marriage. Amen!!*

"Therefore what God has joined together, let no man separate." - Mark 10:9

Day 1: After reading today's devotional and scripture journal about the similarities in your marriage or if you're not married what you would like your marriage to look.
Day 2: Ephesians 5:25
Day 3: Genesis 2:24
Day 4: Song of Songs 8:6-7
Day 5: Ephesians 4:2-3
Day 6: Colossians 3:14
Day 7: Ecclesiastes 4:9-12

Write down one thing each day that you are thankful for.

Week 50: Identity – Who am I?

Several years ago, a friend shared this story with me. A man was found beaten very badly behind a Burger King in Georgia. He was bloody and unconscious, so they took him to the hospital and he eventually woke up. They found out that he had total amnesia and he didn't know who it was. Dr. Phil found out about it and had him on the show. Dr. Phil hired an investigator to try to find out who the guy was but had no luck; nobody came forward to claim they knew him, and the nurse that took care of him in the hospital actually took him in and has been taking care of him. For many years since then, he still has no idea who he is, or who he was before this. Right now, you know your past, your present, and you have a plan for the future, but what if something happened today, something traumatic, and you woke up tomorrow morning not knowing who you are? Imagine waking up and everything from your past is gone. You don't know who you are, you don't know who your friends are, you don't know who your family is, you don't know anything. You're lost and confused. That is exactly what Satan tries to do to you each and every day. Satan uses people. Satan uses the media. Satan uses pain and hurt. Satan puts thoughts in your mind- YOU control your thoughts but others suggest thoughts. When a good thought comes into our head we call it inspiration. When Satan suggests thoughts we call it temptation. Satan wants you to repeat what he tells you - WORDS ARE POWERFUL.

The word Christian is only used a few times in the Bible, but "You are in Christ" is written about 140 times.

"Not only do we know God by Jesus Christ alone, but we know ourselves only by Jesus Christ. We know life and death only through

Jesus Christ. Apart from Jesus Christ, we do not know what is our life, nor our death, nor God, nor ourselves." - Blaze Pascal

"But you are not like that, for you are a chosen people. You are royal priests, a holy nation, God's very own possession. As a result, you can show others the goodness of God, for he called you out of the darkness into his wonderful light. Once you had no identity as a people; now you are God's people. Once you received no mercy; now you have received God's mercy." - 1 Peter 2:9-10 NLT

Who do we say we are? Who do others say we are? Who does God say we are? YOU CONTROL YOU. C.S. Lewis noted that if we saw how glorious we all really are as creations of God, we would be tempted to bow down and worship the very people we slander.

Read and Journal.
Day 1: Corinthians 6:19
Day 2: Ephesians 5:8
Day 3: Philippians 3:20
Day 4: Colossians 2:10
Day 5: Colossians 3:12
Day 6: 1 Thessalonians 1:4
Day 7: Psalms 139:14

Write down one thing each day that you are thankful for.

Week 51: I Am a Work in Progress

What does that even mean? Have you ever scrolled through Instagram, TikTok, Facebook, or any other social media platform and desired to be like someone else? To be as funny as they are, to speak smoothly like they do, to have a talent like they do, to create content that seems to be changing lives according to the amount of followers they have? Yes? Me too!! I actually hate that about myself. I hate that I feel less than when I see someone else so effortlessly doing their thing when I am over here feeling like Moses who can barely spit out a sentence that makes any kind of sense at all. I find myself being envious of others, and I hate it. I hate it because I know I am not supposed to be seeking what others have, the counterfeit of me, and trying to take that and make it who I am. It's not who I am, and I am still in search of who I am in Christ after all these years, and I am over 50 years old. Will I ever achieve it? Will I ever feel whole and content in what God has given me? Do I carry things within me that others think are unique or cool? Does anyone want to be like me? Why do we think this way? Why do we always want to be something other than what we are? I preach against this behavior to the girls I mentor, I tell them to seek God and believe what and who God says they are. So what is my problem? Why am I struggling with myself? Why am I afraid that I am not enough for others, and quite honestly, why do I care? Where is God while I fight my own flesh?

Well, I am glad you asked. He is patiently sitting next to me, reminding me of who I am. Reminding me of how He made me, reminding me that the encouraging words I do speak to people are more than seeds, they are small moments of life change in another's life. My heart is to spread the gospel, to tell people of the goodness of God. To share my testimony and show unbelievers that what God has done for me is real. God changed my life. The enemy is just trying to distract me from the mission, to get me off track and to focus on things that do not matter. So here I sit as I write this, knowing that my past is my testimony, that the struggles I have overcome will help someone else, and that's really all I care about. I don't care if my words are sloppy or messy as long as you can hear my heart on paper (or digitally depending on how you, Reader, are reading it.)

God is always with you, just like He was always with me in the good, the bad, and the unreal situations I have gotten myself into up to this point. So as I write the last devotionals of this book, I pray that these stories have reached your hand, have made you think, maybe even changed your life. Then laying it all out there will be worth it. Everything I have endured, every mortifying mistake I have made, and every good, right choice I picked along the way was for you. As I said before, this book is to you, from me, written from the bottom of my heart. I hope that it has helped you along the way to know that you are not the sum of what you have done but that you are loved yesterday, today, and tomorrow.

Psalms 139:14 says. "For it was you who created my inward parts; you knit me together in my mother's womb. I will praise you because I have been fearfully and wonderfully made." Ephesians 2:10 says, "For we are his handiwork, created in Christ Jesus for good works, which God prepared beforehand, that we should walk in them." Genesis 1:27 says, "So God created man in his own image, in the image of God he created him; male and female he created them."\

Am I a little quirky? Yes. Am I different from you? Probably. I am okay with that. God made me the way I am even though the world has tried to destroy that. So I may struggle a little more when trying to complete a thought or remember a word, but I will do it with purpose and confidence because He is always with me in every circumstance. And He is with you, too!

Read and Journal.
Day 1: Psalms 139:14
Day 2: Ephesians 2:10

Day 3: Genesis 1:27
Day 4: John 10:27-28
Day 5: 1 John 3:2
Day 6: Romans 1:7
Day 7: Romans 6:6

Write down one thing a day that you are thankful for.

Week 52: Straighten Your Crown

Wow, you did it! This is the last devotional in this book. I would like to thank you for reading and studying along with me. You made it through 52 devotionals. 365 days this last year you've devoted to God. Spending time with Him every single day. What an amazing accomplishment. I hope that my life stories have impacted you in a positive way. Some were funny, some were sad, some were life-changing, some were utterly ridiculous, and some gave hope. I pray that the things that I've been through, the lessons that I've learned along the way and the relationship I found with God has helped you a little bit in your journey. Let's remember that every day is a new day. Every day we have a do-over. Every day we have a chance to make a difference in someone's life, in our own life, in a stranger's life. Let's remember when we get up in the morning and we look at ourselves in the mirror that we straighten our crown. That our hearts are in a posture for learning. There have been many times throughout my life that I've had to straighten out my crown. You've read 52 of them. 52 times I've had to re-examine who I am, who God says I am. And I've had to straighten my crown.

We all have a crown, because we are all royalty, those who believe in Him. When that voice comes along and tries to instill fear in me, it's in those moments that I have to take that thought captive, straighten my crown, and press on toward what God is calling me into. When there are choices to be made, right and wrong decisions, times that my words are going to make a difference for either good or bad, those are the times that I need to remind myself who I am, because my words and what I do will either build a palace for me to live in or I'm going to build a prison to be trapped in.

145

When you know who you are, it doesn't matter who you are not. I use this often in my everyday relationships. If we love someone, we will remind them who they are in God. If I'm talking to someone and they're just negative, and they're bitter, instead of correcting them, I'll simply ask them a question. I'll ask, "Are you building a palace for yourself or are you building a prison?" It's a simple question. Please remember that. Write it down somewhere so you see that every day.

•The words you speak will build a palace or a prison.

•When you know who you are, it doesn't matter who you are not.

"But whoever is united with the Lord is one with him in spirit." - 1 Corinthians 6:7

"I will praise you, for I am fearfully and wonderfully made. Marvelous are your works, and I know this very well." - Psalms 139:14

Read and Journal.
Day 1: Romans 6:6
Day 2: Genesis 1:27
Day 3: Jeremiah 1:5
Day 4: 1 Corinthians 12:27
Day 5: 1 Peter 2:9
Day 6: Galatians 3:27-28
Day 7: 1 Corinthians 6:19-20

Write down 1 thing a day from here on out that you are thankful for. Writing down things that we are thankful for helps remind us that we are blessed, even in times that have sorrow. There is always something to be thankful for.

"And all my life You have been faithful

And all my life You have been so, so good

With every breath that I am able

Oh, I'm gonna sing of the goodness of God"

Goodness of God - Bethel Music

Made in the USA
Coppell, TX
06 April 2024

30976802R10090